THE NEW BASKETRY

THE NEW BASKETRY

ED ROSSBACH

 VAN NOSTRAND REINHOLD COMPANY
New York   Cincinnati   Toronto   London   Melbourne

Front.

Barbara Shawcroft in her studio talking
with the author.

Facing Contents: Detail of photograph
page 40.

Printed in the United States of America
Designed by Loudan Enterprises

Published in 1976 by Van Nostrand Reinhold
Company
A Division of Litton Educational Publishing, Inc.
450 West 33rd Street
New York, NY 10001

Van Nostrand Reinhold Limited
1410 Birchmount Road
Scarborough, Ontario M1P 2E7, Canada

Van Nostrand Reinhold Australia Pty. Ltd.
17 Queen Street
Mitcham, Victoria 3132, Australia

Van Nostrand Reinhold Company Ltd.
Molly Millars Lane
Wokingham, Berkshire, England

16 15 14 13 12 11 10 9 8 7 6 5 4 3 2 1

Library of Congress Cataloging in Publication Data

Rossbach, Ed.
  The new basketry.

  Bibliography: p.
  Includes index.
  1. Basket making. I. Title.
TT879.B3R67   746.4   76-4450
ISBN 0-442-27055-0

ACKNOWLEDGMENTS

The University of California has been generous in
supporting my research and making available the remarkable resources of this institution, especially its
libraries and collections.

I thank Lillian Elliott, Joanne Brandford, and Lia Cook
for directing me to artists whose work was unfamiliar
to me; Susan Jamart, Miriam Plotnicov, and Lea Van P.
Miller for directing me to textual material; Emile Bernat
and Sons Co. for allowing me to quote from their inval-
uable publications; and all those artists who provided
me with photographs and who allowed me to photograph their own work or work in their possession. And
I thank my wife for her advice and assistance in the
photography and presentation of the visual material.

PHOTO CREDITS

Page:
31 (bottom) Samuel A. Santiago; 32 Clayton J. Price; 34
(top) Ricco; 50 Ferdinand Boesch; 55 P. Richard Eells;
56 David Cordoni; 80 (top) Demetre Lagios; 99 Jeffrey
Silverthorne

Recently an old basketmaker was asked what she thought of the new baskets being exhibited alongside her traditional work. She replied with scorn, "*What* baskets?" But when a new basketmaker was asked how she felt about being identified with the traditional work, she expressed pleasure; yet, she confessed, she found her own baskets more interesting.

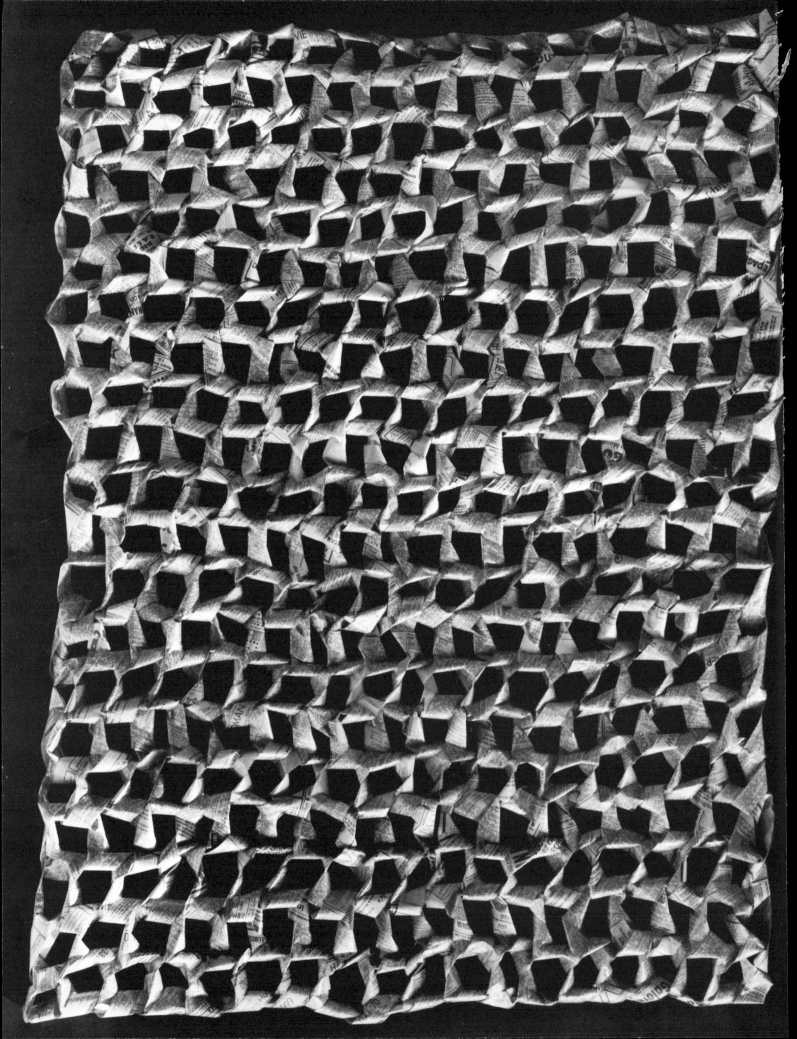

CONTENTS

THE NEW BASKETRY

Fiber is an art medium without conditions. That is the message of the current revolution in hand textiles.

In the 1950s an upheaval occurred in handweaving. It was so fundamental that it is still stirring all the fiber arts, even those which were then little known and seldom practiced.

Certain handweavers stopped thinking of themselves as craftsmen or designers and began to regard themselves as *artists* using fiber for individual expression. They were unwilling to be limited by a single method such as weaving, or by a piece of equipment such as a loom, or by a kind of product such as furnishing fabric. They insisted upon using fiber in any traditional or untraditional way for their own expressive purposes. Their textiles were to be self-sufficient, not conforming to utilitarian needs, color schemes, architectural spaces, or any other extrinsic conditions.

As clearly as possible the work of these weavers declared itself to be one-of-a-kind, nonutilitarian, nondecorative—not a hobby activity and not a reconstruction from the past. In what seemed outrageous fashion, the woven pieces often violated all accepted standards of craftsmanship and tastefulness which had come to characterize good handwoven fabrics.

These artists in fiber—these "fiberworkers"—reacted against the narrowness of previous work in handweaving. They started to explore the entire fiber spectrum, from the most prestigious to the most humble, from tapestry through rope-making. A fiberworker was free to work in many directions, to turn from one method to another for whatever suited his expression. He could make lace or felt or barkcloth or cardweaving or paper.

All the hand methods for working fiber were reviewed and, also, reassembled. Attempts were made to abandon the rigid hierarchies which had fractured the arts and crafts. Connections between the various divisions, isolated by centuries of specialists and specialization, were clarified.

In the textile hierarchy, certain mediums and methods were less valued than others. Basketry held a modest position. At the start of the twentieth century, when a flurry of interest occurred in basketry, one writer observed that basketry had been "reduced among civilized peoples to an insignificant place among the crafts although early in history it had occupied a most important position." Alas, after this enthusiasm for basketmaking subsided, basketry continued to retain its insignificant status.

For many years and in many parts of the world (not only in industrialized societies) basketry was separated from the other textile activities. It was a relatively self-sufficient craft, unlike weaving, which relied on other textile artisans—the spinners, dyers, fullers, etc. Basketry had its own tools and working conditions, its own materials and skills, and it satisfied needs quite unlike those met by the soft textiles of weaving, knitting, lace, and embroidery. Basketmaking existed untouched by influences which were of such consequence in determining the ever-changing character of those other textiles. Since products of basketry tended to be for local consumption rather than for distant markets, the commercial involvements of basketmakers were of a different order—of less consequence economically—than those of weavers. The gulf between basketmaking and other textile skills was widened further when the other textile processes were mechanized while basketry remained a hand process, impervious to change. Baskets stood alone, left over from a hand culture. That they were textiles was more or less forgotten except in academic classifications of the technologies.

The conditions which fostered conservatism in basketmaking allowed baskets to attain refinement through long experimentation. Traditional baskets which were developed for utilitarian, everyday purposes could appear forever direct and assured even after the original purposes were forgotten. Old basketmakers taught the correct ways to young basketmakers in an endless transmittal of established ways. The problems of starts, joinings, and endings had been solved long ago. Such baskets remain completely satisfying for their craftsmanship, their sensitive uses of materials, and the logic of their structure.

The new fiberworkers, in surveying all the uses of flexible fiber, took a fresh look at baskets. The structural relationships to the other textile arts were obvious. The mere adoption of the term "fiber arts" helped restore basketry to its place among textiles. The word "fiberwork" emphasized fiber and fibrousness rather than a technique such as weaving or a product such as a piece of cloth. Whereas a basket does not meet the generally accepted definition of a textile, a basket is immediately acknowledged to be a fiber construction.

Although the new fiberworkers heralded baskets as three-dimensional uses of fiber in tune with the new impulses, the traditional basketmakers continued to maintain their isolation from other textile activities. They had no pretensions of being artists; they were craftsmen producing utilitarian and decorative pieces to earn a livelihood. The traditional basketmakers did not become active in the new movement; indeed they were probably unaware of it, for they were separated from the new fiberworkers by a gulf as wide as that which separates industrial textile technicians from the makers of art fabrics.

New baskets began to be made by weavers. Unlike all the basketry which preceded it, *a new basketry arose out of handweaving.* Basketry and the other textile arts which for so many years had gone separate ways were brought together.

1

A French basketmaker's workshop in the 1750s, as illustrated in Diderot's *Encyclopedia*. Workers are constructing a basketry figure of a Roman soldier. Throughout history the materials and techniques of basketry have been used to create far more than baskets—shelters, masks, fences, furniture, toys, ceremonial objects. (Reproduced through the courtesy of the Bancroft Library, University of California, Berkeley.)

Although baskets have always been very common, very abundant, and very useful, basketmaking is seldom described or even mentioned in writing. Fortunately, when handweaving was at its zenith of technical advance and quantity production, just before the industrial revolution, Diderot, the French philosopher, compiled his *Encyclopedia, or Analytical Dictionary of the Sciences, Arts, and Trades*. In a series of precise and detailed drawings, the *Encyclopedia* shows the complex tools and equipment of hand-spinning and handweaving in eighteenth-century France. Alongside the drawings of airy weaving studios with their mechanical equipment is a drawing of a windowless cellar where the basketmaker worked and probably also lived. His equipment is little more than the simplest bench and a bucket, and a few hand tools. The edges of the room are stacked with hampers and storage baskets, while the floor is strewn with willows ready to be worked. The contrast between weaving and basketmaking was extreme even while both were hand technologies.

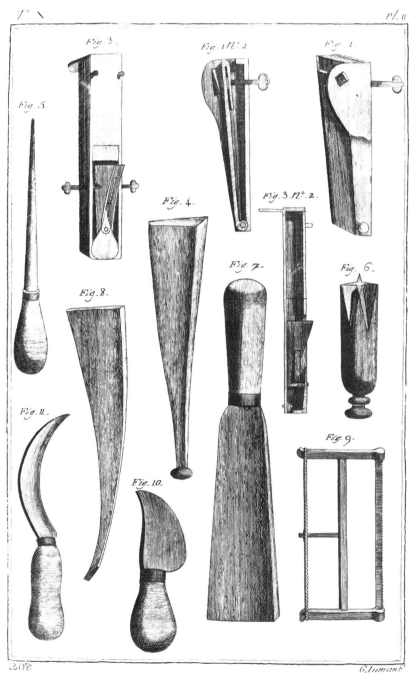

Vannier, Outils.

2

One of several life-size basketry figures, plaited in Mexico, which stand like cigar-store Indians in front of a souvenir shop in Scottsdale, Arizona.

3

Some of the basketmaking tools illustrated in Diderot's *Encyclopedia*. Simple saws, knives, awls, and planes were the basic tools at the same time that complex mechanisms were the tools of weaving, making possible the sumptuous brocades and velvets of the period. (Reproduced through the courtesy of the Bancroft Library, University of California, Berkeley.)

Cole's *Encyclopedia of Dry Goods*, published in the United States in 1900, described the standard fabrics and related merchandise including baskets. The process of making baskets was the same as before but the work was practiced less generally—that is, certain areas of the world specialized in the production. Baskets from these areas were standardized in shape, size, and styles, for distant markets. The baskets were like mass-produced machine-made products except that they were made by hand. The author of the 1900 *Encyclopedia* states that "although basketweaving is as old as history itself, it was not until recently that it had any record as a commercial industry." He says that the only tools used were short knives which were kept very sharp; awls for punching holes; and a "beater" or hammerlike instrument for bending the willow rods. There were no great factories or moneyed proprietors. The work was strictly a home or family industry. "Many whole families, including father, mother and children, did not make to exceed $5 a week." At that time the ornamental sewing baskets, wastebaskets, workbaskets, etc., which were used in American households came from Germany, "our native manufacturers never having been able to compete with the low-priced labor of Bavaria."

The change which occurred—the rapid transition from local production of baskets to specialized production for a world market—is demonstrated by events in the Philippine Islands, where so many of the world's baskets are made today. Following the Spanish-American War in 1898, the Islands were governed by the United States. A strong tradition of basketmaking existed, with a variety of baskets for local everyday use. People who lived in rural and mountain areas with plentiful materials made the baskets which were used in the towns. A few baskets were shipped from one locality to another, especially in the provinces around Manila, but production was small and sales were limited.

As part of the United States government policy to help the Filipinos enter the economic field and take their place in the world's market, schools were established with basketry part of the curriculum in industrial production. At first the baskets made in the schools were practically the same as those used in the children's homes. But then a change occurred. Some of the American teachers who had been brought to the Islands and who were required to teach basketry even though they were untrained in the craft, obtained books from the United States. The only ones available dealt with American Indian basketry. The Filipino students were taught to copy the designs, shapes, and methods described in these books. As the demand for education increased, instruction was gradually turned over to Filipino teachers working under the supervision of the Americans. The Filipino teachers reintroduced the making of native baskets, so that in the schools the handcrafts began to show "an admixture of both the Occidental and the Oriental types." For a while no two baskets were alike; the materials were not uniform; the colors were gaudy. The baskets were often "fearfully and wonderfully made." Much of the work was judged by those in charge of the program to be original but of doubtful value.

To impose some order and control, changes in the instruction began to occur about 1910. Circulars and bulletins for classroom use were issued giving specific instructions. Different materials were introduced with directions for their preparation and use. The goal was uniform methods and standardization of output. This was to be achieved through the use of diagrams, blueprints, blocks and forms. The method was antithetical to traditional ways of learning and producing basketry, when an apprentice worked alongside a basketmaker, or a child worked alongside his parent. The know-how was to be transmitted in a classroom and practiced in factory-like situations. At the same time, efforts were

4

Students at the Philippine Normal School learning to make baskets for the American market. (From *The Philippine Craftsman*, January, 1913.)

made to preserve the old decorative motives from earlier Filipino basketry. Basketmaking as the production of sieves, strainers, fishtraps, fish baskets, and winnowing baskets for local use changed to basketmaking as the production of wastebaskets, sewing baskets, stationery trays, and pin baskets for world markets. The work was approached for its commercial value. Like Bavaria, the Philippines turned out whatever would sell, using a wide variety of materials and techniques, and conforming to standards established somewhere else. The production process was mechanical without being mechanized. Basketry was made to conform to a machine society.

5

Filipinos were taught how to produce baskets of shapes and sizes to satisfy American taste. The uniformity of the work was attributed to standardization of methods and centralized supervision. Handmade products became uniform and interchangeable, like the machine-made goods of American industry. (From *The Philippine Craftsman*, August, 1916.)

16

While basketmaking was becoming a hand process for nonindustrialized areas, weaving had been turned dramatically into a machine process which the industrialized nations attempted to reserve for themselves and which they pursued with greatest diligence and ruthlessness. The new machinery produced such quantities of goods that the markets of nonindustrialized areas could be flooded with cheap machine-made textiles. By imitating the appearance of the goods which the local populations were accustomed to, machine-made merchandise was able to drive out the local handweaving.

The industrialized nations turned out weavings to satisfy the nonindustrialized areas while the nonindustrialized areas turned out baskets to satisfy the industrialized nations. Each—the industrialized product and the nonindustrialized product—showed the marks of the other, and in a curious way conformed to the other.

By the early part of the present century then, both basketmaking and weaving were centralized and specialized activities producing goods for world markets. The critical difference between the two was that basketmaking was a hand process relegated to underdeveloped areas, while the weaving was a highly mechanized process reserved for the industrialized nations.

The marked contrast can be viewed in another way. Before the industrial revolution when the steadily increasing demand for more fabrics far outstripped the capabilities of the hand-spinners and weavers, the need was for either a speeded-up process or a different product which could satisfy the same needs. During the early industrial revolution the first solution—the speeding-up of the process—was found in power looms and power spinning. More recently, however, the other solution—the different product to satisfy the same needs—has also been found. Industrialization is no longer a matter of converting hand processes to machine processes, but is a matter of devising new processes altogether. Man-made extruded yarns are being substituted for traditional yarns. Knit, nonwoven, and molded fabrics are being substituted for woven cloth. To a remarkable extent weaving, which is a relatively slow process even when performed by power machines, is being replaced by knits which are faster, and by nonwoven fabrics which are even faster.

Since basketmaking was not susceptible to mechanization, the problem of producing more and more was temporarily solved by concentrating production and by standardizing hand methods in areas of the world where labor was cheap. Today other products which can be produced by power methods are being substituted for baskets.

In a sense then, what has happened to weaving and basketry over several centuries can be viewed as surprisingly the same. At first new ways were found to produce the old products more quickly. Then new products were found as substitutes. This substitution process which is now underway has profound implications not only for commercial weaving and basketmaking but for handweaving and art basketmaking. At the present stage in the history of the craft movement, what is produced commercially is a determining factor in what is considered worth producing by hand.

When steam and water power were first applied to spinning and weaving, no one could have predicted that the notion was being generated that fiber and the machine are inextricably bound. The early industrial revolution, which was concerned with speeding the manufacture of cotton goods in Great Britain, became so identified with fiber that it is known today as the textile phase (1780–1840). The takeover of textile production by power equipment was so sudden and virtually total that in a remarkably short time the word "woven" came to mean "power woven." Handweaving was soon considered anachronistic, virtually meaningless in a machine society. For a while none of the hand processes for making soft textiles—except tapestry—seemed worth perpetuating as providing a superior or different product.

The gains of mechanization were more apparent than any losses. Satisfaction and a sense of confidence were found in the increase of goods and in the machine product itself and in the machine.

In most obvious and also in most subtle ways, the dimensions of fiber in industrial societies quickly became severely restricted to what was feasible for machine production. Uses of fiber which resisted mechanization—such as basketry—tended to become the province of unmechanized societies. If a hand technique for constructing with fiber could not be mechanized, another technique was made to suffice or another product was substituted for the original.

As mechanization became identified with fiber in the early phase of the industrial revolution, fiber became identified with mechanization. Fiber became an industrial material to be used in ways compatible with machine production. Fiber processes were machine processes. Upon fiber was imposed the uniformity which came to be a hallmark of a machine product.

By the late nineteenth and early twentieth centuries, power-woven textiles had replaced most handwoven textiles in Europe and America. The old handlooms, previously so numerous and widespread, had been dismantled and destroyed. The power weaving was done in vast mills, out of sight of the ordinary person. Any handweaving that survived was most often in rural areas of Europe and America, where isolated looms turned out traditional folk fabrics.

When enough time had passed since the takeover by power equipment, handweaving could be viewed by urban dwellers as a novelty, something interesting, unassociated with the humdrum task it had once been. Attempts could then be made to re-establish and revive the handcrafts, after "machinery and steam had well-nigh crushed them out but in far quarters." The revival of interest in handweaving occurred first in England as part of the Arts and Crafts movement.

This movement in the late nineteenth century is associated with the name of William Morris, although others were also responsible for its inception and development. Morris was a Victorian designer, craftsman, poet, and social reformer. In his youth he had been influenced by the Pre-Raphaelites, who rejected the artificiality of their times and tried to recapture the spirit and ideals of the ages before Raphael. Just as the Pre-Raphaelite brotherhood had done, Morris looked to the past. He felt that when the Renaissance suddenly faded, a chill fell upon the arts. The lesser arts, such as textiles, went downward along with the greater arts of painting and sculpture. Morris believed that until what he called recent times, everything that the hand of man touched was more or less beautiful, so that formerly all people who made anything, as well as all people who used the things, shared in art. Men found pride and satisfaction in their work. He was horrified by the degradation of machine design in Victorian England, and the social changes which had attended the transfer from hand to machine production. He thought that the decline in standards of craftsmanship and in public taste, which had become so obvious by the middle of the nineteenth century, was only the last stage in a long process which began when division of labor replaced the medieval system, whereby everything "was made not merely by hand but by one pair of hands from start to finish." By his writings and teachings, and by the example of his own work (which in retrospect sometimes appears to contradict his utterances), he tried for a while to reverse the irreversible; he attempted to persuade society to abandon its machines and return to an earlier mode of production. He saw salvation in a return to handwork, with the artist-craftsman doing all the steps in the process. To this end, he himself learned to weave, dye, etc. He designed rugs, tapestries, panels for embroidery, wallpaper, fabrics, books—to be made by himself, his associates, and workmen. His goal was to improve the quality of design and the quality of life.

Basketry was not one of the crafts of the early Arts

and Crafts movement, although by the end of the nineteenth century, basketwork was being encouraged in England as a home art or home employment. Since baskets were still produced by hand, no reform was necessary, no magic of hand production was required to restore the satisfactions of hand processes, to return good design to an ancient art. Baskets had not been directly corrupted by the machine although they were to be contaminated by the taste, methods, and changed conditions of the new machine society.

The tendency to look backward which characterized the Arts and Crafts movement is evident in the revival of handweaving and basketmaking which subsequently took place in the United States. Mary Atwater, who was so influential in stimulating interest in handweaving, not only turned to Colonial weaving for inspiration but surprisingly rejected, like the Pre-Raphaelites, "the fussy prettiness of the Late Renaissance."

Otis Mason recalled the message of William Morris by giving a gratuitous title to his great book on Indian basketry, *Studies in a Textile Art Without Machinery.*

Even the handweavers who dominated the American weaving scene in the middle of the present century echoed Morris. For although they were certainly not recommending the rejection of the machine, they deplored the quality of machine design and were zealous in their efforts to improve it through handweaving. Their work was a remarkable expression of the impulses that came to characterize so much of the early Arts and Crafts movement—the missionary zeal, the sense of reform, the imposed value judgments, the heavy sense of responsibility toward the future.

The entire handcraft movement in America during the twentieth century is permeated with the ideas of the British Arts and Crafts movement: belief in the corrupting influence of the machine on design; reverence for early work as purer than later work; regard for the handmade object as superior to the machine-made object; satisfaction in controlling the manufacture from start to finish.

From the annihilation of hand processes the old was gradually reborn as something new, with new purposes and meanings. Wherever it spread the rebirth, known as the Arts and Crafts movement, assumed distinctive forms which evolved in response to diverse conditions.

In the United States, especially in the Southern Highlands, some handcrafts persisted. These lingering traditions exerted positive influences in the early years of the revival of the various skills. Traditional craft objects, sometimes preserved in museum collections, served as prototypes for new handcrafts. Examples were studied and copied, as were the remaining tools and equipment and the ancient ways of using them. Even the old aesthetic standards were adopted.

More remarkable than these remnants of old ways which lingered on in a continent so vast and so sparsely settled were the traces of a totally different culture—one which far more dramatically than that of the Southern Highlanders seemed left over from an almost forgotten past. Unique to America were the handcrafts of the native Americans.

The new railroads which crossed the continent encouraged travelers to view the scenic wonders of the West, and return with souvenirs from trading posts and railroad stations. Genuine Indian baskets and pots were collected as trinkets and curios to decorate china closets and plate rails, while blankets were purchased to be hung on walls or used as throws and rugs. These handmade souvenirs began to appear prominently in machine-made environments. They were able to recall more than the trip west; they evoked a disappearing way of life at the very time that the Arts and Crafts movement was looking backward beyond machine society for lost values. They evoked the American past as surely as did the Colonial coverlets, for always on the edge of the American consciousness was another way of life which the very same land had fostered. The Indian work was clearly handmade, uncontaminated by the machine.

6

Coiled basket, Pima, Arizona. This is one of the kinds of baskets with bold geometric patterning which were imitated during the craze for making "Indian" baskets at the start of the century. (Collection of Robert H. Lowie Museum of Anthropology, University of California, Berkeley.)

The new craftworkers began to copy motives from baskets, pottery, and blankets. Indian patterns were embroidered and stenciled onto wall hangings and curtains, scarves and table runners; applied as painted decorations onto handmade pottery and wooden shelves and trays; etched in copper bookends and boxes.

As Indian baskets were collected and observed, distinctions in quality became clear. When it was apparent that the finest baskets were the older ones, efforts were made to perpetuate the old work. A surprising result was a craze for making Indian baskets by non-Indians.

7

In the early 1900s there was a craze for making "Indian" baskets. Although traditional techniques, shapes, and motives were imitated, these baskets had their own look because raffia and reed were substituted for the native materials. (From *The Craftsman*, December, 1903.)

Amateur basketmakers carefully imitated Indian baskets, often as a means of preserving the basketry that was vanishing. In a curious desperate effort, the amateur basketmakers attempted to preserve someone else's tradition (which, in a way, was also their tradition), to save the past from the incursions of the machine. The imitations were considered to be "pure Indian"—the exact weaves, the authentic designs. Adapted motives often appeared isolated and forlorn, empty of meaning, incredibly sad, just as they finally appeared on the degenerate but "authentic" Indian baskets.

The imitation baskets were seldom to be mistaken for the genuine old article. The most obvious difference and certainly the easiest to describe was in the materials used. The Indian baskets had evolved from local vegetal material not available to the imitators working in regions as unlike as New England and southern California. Much of the character of the authentic baskets derived from fibers selected and prepared in traditional ways for special qualities of color, texture, strength, and pliability. The handcraft basketmakers substituted materials which were purchasable everywhere and easy to use—easier on the "delicate fingers of the ladies." The change in material imparted a synthetic quality. Something which had developed out of one material was rendered in another material. Baskets became improvisations on Indian baskets.

Raffia and rattan from the tropics became the popular materials for "Indian baskets." Raffia was substituted for the various grasses, while rattan replaced willow and twigs. Rafia was most favored for its clean, tough, flexible strands, which could be vegetable-dyed in reaction against the machine and chemical dyeing. The raffia could also be purchased already dyed in a variety of strong colors. The laborious task of preparation by separating and shredding the layers of the enormous palm leaves had taken place thousands of miles away, probably in Madagascar or the Congo. The strands could be used like sewing thread, with a blunt needle which made it safe for the classroom. Rattan, referred to as reed and wicker, was more difficult since it required manipulations not related to sewing and embroidery, and it was rather messy. It was strongest and most pliable when used damp after being soaked. A further disadvantage was that baskets of reed were not as susceptible as those of raffia to colorful patterning.

Even when specialized materials were obviously essential to the effects they hoped to achieve, the imitators contented themselves with raffia and reed, which became recognizable constants in the work, unifying it.

The willingness to use available, already prepared fiber seems to characterize fiberwork throughout the century. The same materials—the same mercerized cottons, linens, and woolens, the same novelty yarns—are marks of the country's fiberwork at any particular time. Work can be dated by the materials used; they are identifiable by trade name and color name—Lily, Bernat, Maypole, etc. The materials make cohesive a vast body of craftwork produced at one time across the entire country. The insistent appearance of the same machine-made yarns, or even the same handmade yarns (by someone else's hands in Mexico or Guatemala, Greece or Turkey) seems, so far, to characterize fiberwork produced by hand in an industrial society.

In learning basketmaking the young Indians had worked with their elders over a period of years, participating in the gathering expeditions, the preparation of materials, and the basketmaking sessions. The handcraft basketmakers had to learn to use anonymous materials from purchased sets of instructions and how-to-do-it manuals. For a while basketry flourished as an activity for children in the public schools. The teachers often knew little more about basketmaking than did the children. The refinements of the craft could scarcely be transmitted in this way. A trial-and-error approach was required. Although instructions were for specific Indian baskets, all sorts of improvisations occurred in shapes and patterns. The basketmakers were not guided by the utilitarian considerations and the traditions which controlled the shapes and motives of the Indian work. So with their uncertain craftsmanship and foreign materials, and their freedom from traditional restraints, the handcraft basketmakers imparted their own look to their Indian baskets. The results had an innovative, worked-out look, often absent in Indian basketry in which the construction problems had been solved long ago and the solutions perpetuated. The same kind of energy and innovation, and concentration in working materials into shape, were to appear again in the new basketry sixty or seventy years later.

For a while imitating Indian baskets had many enthusiasts. It also had its detractors. In 1910 a reviewer said, "Most amateur basketmakers imitate the Indian forms, designs and weaves, or else do more or less commonplace things with wicker and raffia, so that the majority of baskets made by craftworkers are not only inferior to the Indian work, but even to the ordinary commercial basket." Another critic said, "To imitate the basketry of the North American Indians has recently been the ambition of public school children and the passing fancy of club-women." Indian basketry "has much deeper meaning than has been suspected by the majority of those who have recently counted its stitches and mechanically repeated its symbolic designs in an effort, made without especial reason, to produce objects of no important value or use."

Gradually the impulse toward making Indian baskets subsided. A few craftsman tried to elevate their basketmaking to something more than imitation. Sometimes they attempted to depart from the simple geometric patterns which had evolved so naturally from the techniques of basketmaking and weaving. The other popular patterns of the times, the conventionalized curves of tendrils and waterlily pads, could best be stenciled or painted onto the basketry surface in the same way that they were applied to cloth and other materials. Some workers tried to use native vegetation, devising structures appropriate to the materials. They produced straightforward baskets, simple and unpretentious. When well done, such works were almost indistinguishable from commercial baskets available for a few cents. So while the basketmaker had the satisfaction of making something with his own hands, he confronted the problem which has recurred ever since in the handcrafts in a machine society—is it worth doing something laboriously with one's own hands that can be turned out as well by machine or by cheap hand production?

Basketmaking lingered as a handcraft activity for summer camps and—at least according to tiresome legend—as therapy in mental institutions. A stigma became attached to basketry; it was dismissed as busywork for children and mental defectives. Even so, basketmaking continued to be pursued, although with little recognition, as a modest and satisfying handcraft.

8

A burned reed basket shown in 1903. At the time of the craze for "Indian" basketmaking, the other arts and crafts objects were sometimes decorated with geometric Indian motives, but more often they showed the curved forms of the aesthetic movement. These curves were sometimes applied to baskets with stencils, just as they were applied to curtains, bookcases, etc. (From *The Craftsman*, December, 1903.)

9

"The Gray Bowl," made before 1915. When native grasses were used instead of raffia, the crafts baskets tended toward simplicity and directness, with a vigor and spontaneity. (From *Raffia Basketry as a Fine Art* by Gertrude and Mildred Ashley.)

At the same time that amateur basketmakers were copying Indian baskets, other people were learning to weave by hand, copying the Colonial coverlets which were preserved from America's past, and copying also the overshot patterns still being woven in the Southern Highlands as part of an unbroken tradition. Handweaving was approached as a modern revival of a national popular art.

The "Indian" baskets and the "Colonial" weaving were not considered to be related textile expressions. Basketmaking and handweaving were quite separate handcrafts. Weavers were not also basketmakers; preoccupation with the loom mechanism foreclosed any such explorations as basketry. Even so the pattern weavings and the "Indian" baskets were one in that they found their inspiration in something of recognized value and distinction from the past. Both were attempts to renew a dying tradition.

When these attempts to revive a past tradition failed, only handweaving was able to change, to search for a place in modern society. Colonial or overshot weaving gave way to what came to be known in the nineteen-forties and fifties as Contemporary handweaving to distinguish it from the traditional work and to indicate its relevance to the times. Handweaving was to look forward, not backward; it was to be based on experimentation rather than the reworking of old ideas. It was to face the problems of new conditions and new materials. Handweaving was to find its appropriate role in the machine age through an imaginative rediscovery of fundamentals of processes and materials. And it was to exert an influence—a control—on the machine and its output. Weavings were to be models for industry. They were to appear anonymous rather than as the expression of an individual artist.

In describing Contemporary weaving, two qualities were invariably linked together: color and texture.

Offhand this suggests a stressing of the sensuous aspects of fiber. Looking back now the work seems remarkably nonsensuous, without emotion or individuality. Weavings were direct, straightforward uses of the loom mechanism, with the simplest threading and treadling. Weavers seem to have paid attention to William Morris when he admonished designers, if they had to design for machine-work, "to make it mechanical with a vengeance, at the same time as simple as possible." But the Contemporary weavers seem to have ignored his warning, "don't let yourselves be made machines, or it is all up with you as artists." Creativity and spontaneity were stifled by a drive toward a restrictive functionalism and good machine design.

Contemporary weavers limited themselves to specific categories of fabrics: upholstery, drapery, linen, rugs, and suiting. The category which offered most opportunity for experimentation in materials and techniques was drapery, which included sheer casement cloths. In retrospect it seems that many of the new, experimental wall hangings and tapestries which were to appear in post-Contemporary weaving evolved from casement cloths with their open structures, their isolation of individual yarns as recognizable and distinct structural elements, and their preoccupation with spatial considerations beyond the edges of the cloth.

The other category of Contemporary weaving which led to the art fabric of the 1970s was rugs. As part of the focus on designing utilitarian textiles for the new interiors, weavers made rya or flossa rugs with pile knotted into the warps on the loom. Surfaces became exaggeratedly three-dimensional at a time when textiles were generally regarded as, by nature, flat, planar, two-dimensional. These rugs were referred to as sculptured or sculptural. Being small (their size was determined by the width of a standard loom), they could be dramatic and impractical, all in the name of affording a playful accent for an interior at a time when other fabrics were reserved, off-white, natural, and muted chartreuse.

Rugs became sculptural splotches of color and texture; they seemed splashy, painterly, expressionistic. Weavers even experimented with modifying the outer shape so that many rugs departed from the rectangular to become circles, ovals, and free forms; such departures required inventive solutions to technical problems which were quite foreign to Contemporary weaving.

Making a flossa rug required much handling of fiber. Yarn strands had to be combined and tied into butterflies, then inserted into stretched warps and knotted around the warps. Both warp and pile yarn were constantly being handled during the slow and deliberate—and very modular—process. Techniques such as twining and soumak which were used to vary the regular woven surface required hand manipulation of the yarns. To keep the weaving process within reasonable bounds as far as time was concerned, yarn elements had to be large. Since large-scale weaving elements were not available, weavers had to learn to ply yarns and even to spin fiber. Unlike other textiles, rugs required a termination of the warps by fringing, knotting, and binding. The cut ends of yarn and the long lengths of yarn lying free on the rug surfaces revealed qualities in yarn denied to other Contemporary weavings which were so uniformly devoid of all fringes, tassels, and rawnesses. Not only were the rugs colorful and textural, but they were undeniably sensual and even sexual. They gave the weaver and anyone else who saw or felt the rug a fiber experience.

Rugs seemed to require a considerable expenditure of time and a different involvement in designing, quite unlike organizing three or four yarns into a twill or other simple woven structure. Weavers felt that they had to "put more of themselves into it." Rugs seemed more individual, personal, and expressive than the yard goods of upholstery and drapery. The product seemed more concrete and tangible than a length of drapery or upholstery which was only intended as a design sample.

10

LEA VAN P. MILLER Twined rug, jute, and New Zealand flax. The slow hand manipulation of hard fibers on the loom produced textural effects which were a welcome departure from the machine-like uses of machine-made yarns which characterized the utility textiles of the Contemporary handweavers.

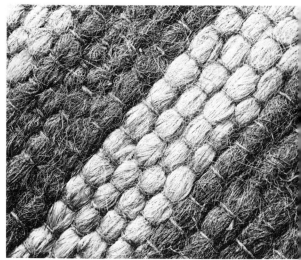

11

GERALDINE FUNK Handwoven rug of coconut cord, coconut fiber, and maguey. This is one of a group of textiles designed for the Puerto Rico Industrial Development Company to foster the use of native fibers of Puerto Rico in modern interiors.

31

Finally, the rugs were not used as rugs at all but were made to be hung on the wall as three-dimensional wall hangings. Despite the fact that the goal of Contemporary handweaving was functionalism appropriate to today's architecture, handweaving was again and again subverted to produce things strictly decorative or strictly expressive. Works kept being produced which were, as Anni Albers said about her own pictorial weavings, "useless, of course, in any practical sense."

Gradually weaving was becoming more clearly three-dimensional, not only as a planar structure to be manipulated three-dimensionally away from the loom, as draperies, upholsteries, and suitings, but three-dimensional while on the loom. The sculptural potentials of weaving were gradually being rediscovered.

12, 13

LENORE TAWNEY "Autumn Song." Loom structures began to be explored for their three-dimensionality. The weaving of natural linen becomes double at the center where it bellies out. Loom techniques of layering which had been used to create structural patterning began to be used three-dimensionally. Wall hangings became more than sculptural reliefs; they were in the round. A new concern for spatial quality began to characterize post-Contemporary fiberwork.

14

GLEN KAUFMAN "Cross of Linen." A looped, knotted pile of natural linen appears on a hand-spun natural wool ground. Wall hangings with vigorous textures and pronounced sculptural effects evolved from utilitarian flossa rugs.

15

Tapestry tunic, Peru, Chimu Culture. The rich sculptural surface of tassels and needle-knitted figures contrasts strongly with some other Peruvian weavings which show to an unusual degree a flat surface devoid of fibrous appearance. With great inventiveness the ancient Peruvians explored the various aspects of textile structure and expressive uses of fiber. (Courtesy of The Brooklyn Museum.)

16

ROBERT SAILORS Screen with wefts
of bamboo and wood slats, and warp of
chenille, metallic braid, and textured yarns.
Traditional materials of basketmaking
appeared conspicuously in contemporary
interiors in conjunction with machine-
made yarns.

A kind of Contemporary handweaving, related spe-
cifically to the new basketry which was soon to appear,
was the woven blinds associated with Dorothy Liebes,
who was a leading Contemporary weaver. She and others,
in their search for solutions to the new architecture's
problems of privacy, light control, etc., found that the
folds and softness of the draperies and casement cloths
often violated the architect's intentions. To replace such
soft textiles, screens or blinds were woven with rigid
elements that retained the planar quality of weavings
under tension on the loom. These rigid elements were
often the hard fibers of basketry and mat-making—
wood, bamboo, rattan, and finally plastic rods. They were
used as wefts which were encircled and gripped by
flexible warps. Industrial yarns appeared in these weavings alongside traditional basketry materials. Since these
woven blinds were extremely popular, as they still are
today, the combination of hard and soft fibers in textiles
became an everyday experience.

Some handweavers began to experiment with reeds,
raffia, tules, pandanus, Hong Kong grass, and willow in
their woven blinds. At first weavers were compelled to
search for materials in basketry supply houses, but soon
hard fibers began to appear in yarn shops. Weavers accepted them as textile components.

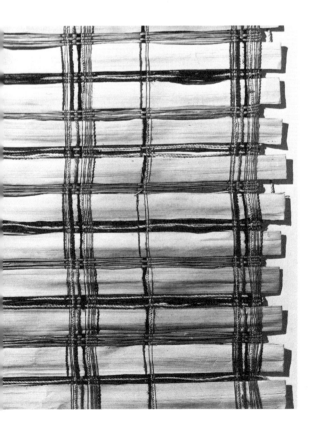

17

LEA VAN P. MILLER Woven screen of
broad pandanus leaves, with raffia, Hong
Kong grass, linen, and chenille. Hard
fibers of basketry and mat-making are
combined with yarns on the loom to
express the natural beauty of the vegetation. The natural elements appear suspended in space.

Although changes in handweaving were occurring slowly, and often privately, the well-established Contemporary weaving continued to dominate. Post-Contemporary weaving, or the new fiberwork, appeared dramatically and emphatically in the fifties as a reflection of postwar values and attitudes in the arts and in society as a whole. The war brought a disillusionment with machine progress, and ended the idealistic zeal to improve mass culture through good design of machine products. It also brought a different awareness of the developing nations and of their cultural contributions; a concern for the environment; a search for renewal in nature; an experimentation with new life-styles; a quest for personal expression and identity by women and minorities.

Weavers of the new fiberwork seemed determined to set aside all the technical niceties which had accrued to handweaving as a ladylike pursuit heavily involved with preserving a valued tradition and zealously concerned with good design and raising standards of machine-made goods. The reaction questioned the weighty, nonjoyous, nonsensuous, nonexpressive dogma of structural soundness as the measure of textile quality, and dispensed with the persistent touchstone, the machine.

The focus of handweaving shifted in the fifties from what the machine could do to what the machine could *not* do. The new weavings were self-sufficient. Their justification was not in a possible influence on something else, any more than the justification of the pursuit of handweaving was, as the Bauhaus once thought, in its providing structural training for work in architecture. Weavers concentrated on processes that were most conspicuously *hand* processes. Those processes which had resisted mechanization had a special appeal. Weavers turned away from work that was anonymous and impersonal. When their work was least machine-like, the handweavers were most certain that it was truly a free personal expression.

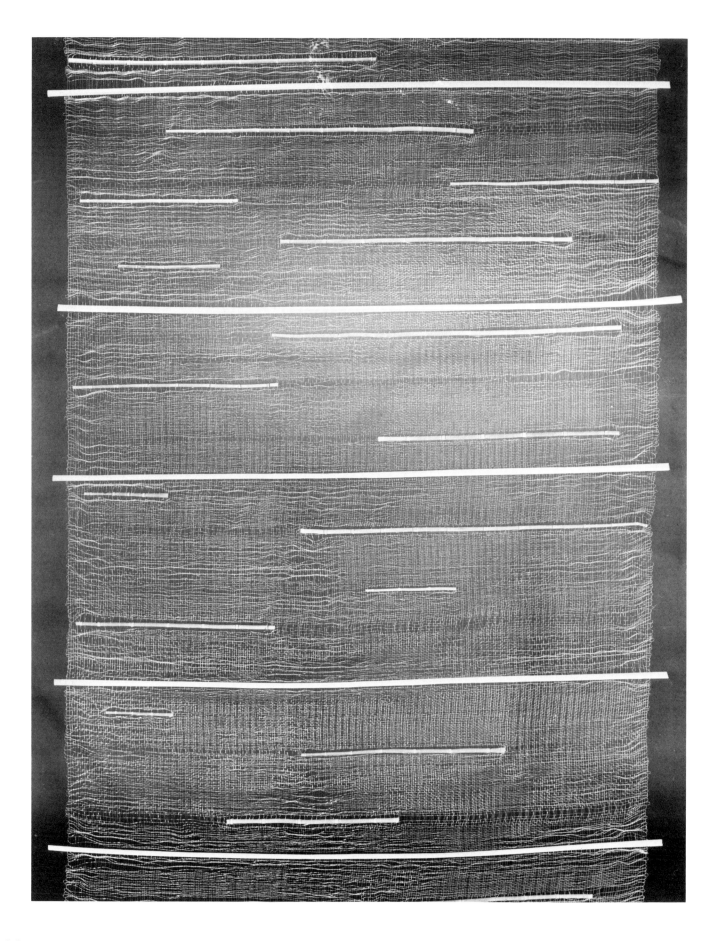

Although the upheaval in handweaving occurred in many small ways and was the result of many weavers "experimenting," stretching the rules to accept more and more, the change was announced most clearly by the appearance of a kind of wall hanging totally unrelated to the machine's potential. Frail, irregular warps were traversed uncertainly by wefts which strayed in unpredictable and whimsical fashion here and there in the web without repeat from start to finish. Sometimes branches and seed pods were entangled as unlikely wefts in flimsy warps. Sometimes everything seemed ready to disintegrate. Feathers, shells, sequins, eucalyptus buds— all manner of materials were inserted precariously into the web. The weavings seemed temporary, transitory, not made to last. They were often disintegrating before they could be attached to the wall. Obviously the emphasis was not on utility or structural soundness.

18

Facing page:
THELMA BECHERER Tapestry, 1956. Handwoven clear green plastic with dried reeds, 110" × 34". This was among the most adventurous handwoven textiles shown by The Museum of Modern Art in their 1956 exhibition of contemporary American work produced by industry and craftsmen, "Textiles USA." In the catalog Arthur Drexler says that the craftsman when not designing for machine production is free to explore "pure" textile design. Drexler selects this textile by Thelma Becherer as perhaps the most interesting example of such exploration. He describes it as "utterly useless," and adds, "Fragile and curiously poetic, this work deserves to be admired in itself, like an ornamental vase." (Collection, The Museum of Modern Art, New York. Gift of the artist.)

19

LENORE TAWNEY "Shore Bird" (detail). In a widely spaced delicate warp, the weft moves as in eccentric tapestry but is beaten so loosely that both warp and weft assert their linear nature while the feathers are left to lie on the surface as feathers.

Appearing as it did alongside the well-established Contemporary weaving, the new work seemed shockingly personal, emotional, introspective, and moody—the kind of expression which had long been absent from textiles and which suggested the impact of painting and sculpture. Indeed the new weavers were often painters and sculptors attempting to approach the use of fiber with the same directness and freedom with which they approached the use of paint and other mediums.

Somehow the new wall hangings placed a new emphasis on fiber. Yarns seemed to assert their individual fibrous identity rather than to appear as anonymous participants. Yarns moved through open structures. They were traceable from beginning to end. Sometimes they functioned structurally and sometimes not. The works seemed a declaration of yarn—of fiber—manipulated for an aesthetic purpose. Fiber was perceived anew.

Fiber satisfies so many everyday needs. Everyone knows what it is and how reasonably it should be used.

This general familiarity encouraged a remarkable conservatism and resistance to change, both in and out of the textile industry. The unconscious resistances and the invented boundaries created for everyone working with fiber a climate both arid and stultifying.

During the forties Anni Albers advocated a return to material in its original state. She said we had become so overgrown with information that we had neglected our formative impulse. She thought that by experiencing material and participating in the stages of change we would know the adventure of being close to the stuff the world is made of and would recover a sense of directness. Yet the exploration of material by the Contemporary weavers was in using preformed yarn, finding what it would do, what its properties and potentialities were. Creativity was expressed in the selection and organization of tested yarns within a predetermined structure of horizontal and vertical elements intersecting at right angles.

When the new fiberworkers approached the handling

of raw fiber they often had only the most makeshift tools and the sketchiest information. Their methods were quite haphazard. All was an act of discovery. The experience, the sense of wonder and enjoyment, were primary even when a product happened to result. If all that was wanted was yarn, it was obtainable at the store, often far more cheaply.

In working with fiber in its raw state and even when transforming yarn into fabric, the fiberworkers attempted to approach the work without preconceptions—free of the onerous rules which had controlled fiberwork for so long. Fiber was played with and manipulated. Rules were disregarded. The ways were to be determined afresh. The new fiberworkers wanted their ways to be consistent with the materials and equipment available to them, the amount of time they were willing to spend, and their own standards of a result. While they admired and were inspired by such textiles as the tapa cloths of Oceania, the felt of the Russian steppes, and the embroidery of Rajasthan, they did not adopt the standards which governed these works.

The new fiberworkers found pleasure in the processes themselves. By doing everything—not only that small part of textile construction which Anni Albers had described as the "imaginative" part—they began to rediscover the sense of totality of the textile arts, lost and distorted when concentration was solely on designs for weaving.

20

Tapa cloth tunic, Pago Pago, Tutuila, Samoa. The tapa cloth is cut into a tunic shape, painted with patterns, and embellished with cut fringes. The fringed fiber, glossy with the applied color, creates a lively, sensuous textile. (Collection of Robert H. Lowie Museum of Anthropology, University of California, Berkeley.)

21

Tapa cloth, Pago Pago, Tutuila, Samoa. Tapa cloth, which is usually thought of as a surface for patterns, was also used in a sculptural way, with the fiber itself the conspicuous feature. Unfamiliar fibers and ways of creating textiles with them— other than by converting them into yarn— interested the new fiberworkers. (Collection of Robert H. Lowie Museum of Anthropology, University of California, Berkeley.)

24

ED ROSSBACH "The Morning Paper." Newspaper is used as a textile fiber, rolled into linear elements and then manipulated into knotless netting.

22

MARY WINDER BAKER Felt Bundle. Natural dark and white wool is arranged in patterns to create a sheet of felt. The new fiberworkers are exploring the making of felt and paper, discovering for themselves the remarkable potentials of patterning and forming.

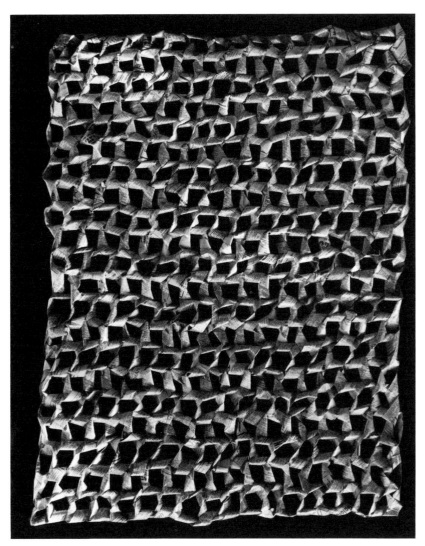

23

MARY WINDER BAKER Felt Bundle. The wool fiber retains the appealing texture of fiber fresh from the carders.

25

SUE VENTURINO Plaited Construction (detail). Strips of rags and graph paper are plaited together to establish a visual relationship between the horizontal-vertical grid of the woven structure of the rags, and the horizontal-vertical applied grid of the graph paper. The plaiting, instead of being kept flat as it could have been, is loosely rolled and meshed for a three-dimensional effect.

26

MARY DE BONE Crocheted Dome (in progress). Hand-spun cotton covers a wooden frame. The soft fibers of weaving create a colorful structure, providing a visual experience from both inside and out.

27

Zulu hut in construction showing framework, South Africa. The skeleton will be covered with other fibers. Fibers worked in basketry techniques have been used for many centuries to create dwellings. (Courtesy of the American Museum of Natural History.)

28

TED HALLMAN Solar Environment,
photographed at the Oakland Art Museum, Oakland, California. Acrylic yarns
are knotted on a steel armature, and
fringes attached.

Certainly the handling of raw material sharpened awarenesses. Fiber appeared in a variety of guises, changing in glossiness, hardness, strength, color as it became a linear element. By carding, twisting, and plying, fiber-workers organized the multitude of disparate fibers from the unknown state to the familiar form. In the process they comprehended fiber. Each aspect which fiber assumed was intriguing. Weavers saw potentialities in fiber not only as yarn but as fleece and rollags and roving. Ways had to be found to incorporate such fiber into works. It was tied in as pile, trapped as bundles along with weft yarns, laid in painstakingly in open warps.

29

GLEN KAUFMAN "Dark Moon." The inlaid wool fiber suggests a fleece, contrasted with the flat tapestry moon and the fringe.

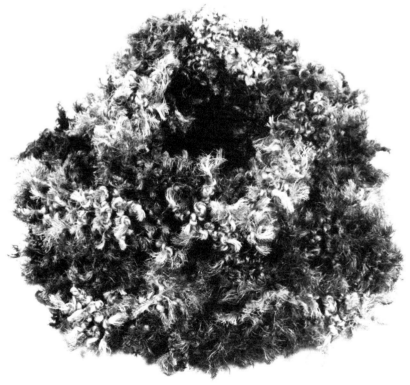

30

CAROLINE VON KLEECK BEARD Basket of red, yellow, and blue sisal twine. The knots and raveled ends create a sensuous color/fiber object.

31, 32

Wiglet of cassowary feathers, New Guinea Highlands. The feathers are densely packed over a fiber structure. The foundation structure is a beautiful organization of fiber firmly holding the feathers. (Private collection.)

Awareness of fiber came about in ways other than by handling raw materials and constructing yarns and ropes. For an interaction occurred: working with raw material led to the use of techniques other than weaving, while the hand manipulation required in these other techniques led to tactile and visual responses to fiber itself. In techniques such as macramé and square knotting, no implement or tool separated the worker from his material. Fiber constantly moved through his fingers. Even weaving provided new fiber experiences when weavers turned to techniques which had not interested the Contemporary weaver because they were not machine-like and were quite unrelated to designing for industry. Thus, when fiberworkers began to investigate a traditional weaving technique such as ikat, they increased fiber awareness.

33

Netted bag, Andaman Islands. Fiber netting is hung with shells. (Collection of the American Museum of Natural History.)

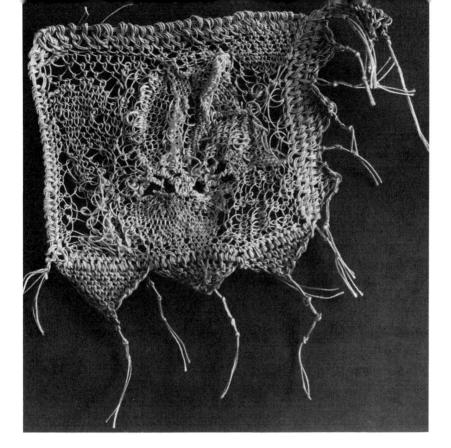

34

JOANNE BRANDFORD Lace. The fabric wrinkles and puckers; loops lift from the surface; yarn ends hang free almost as a fringe, making lace clearly a fibrous construction rather than only a pattern of lines.

35

LILLIAN ELLIOTT Net. The netting process is a continual hand manipulation of fiber. In the finished net the yarn is suspended in space almost like a free fiber element. Layer upon layer of netting creates a dense textural mass; hundreds of changing space volumes are defined, fitting together into a total volume of great complexity.

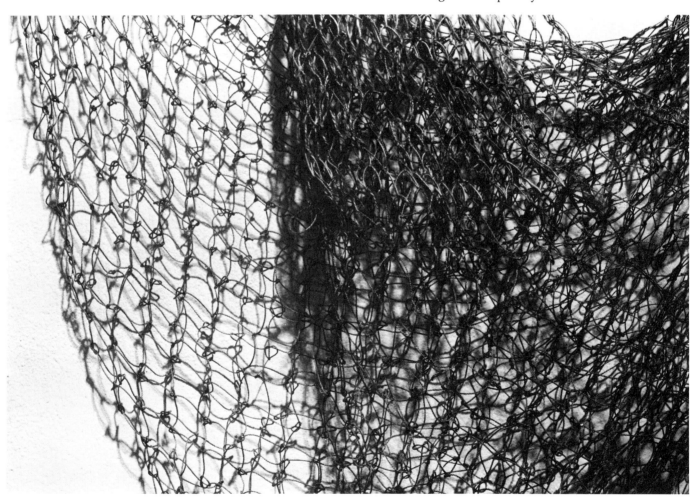

Ikats gave the worker a taste for the beauty of bound and unbound bundles of yarn, an awareness of the energy of the skein and the energy of the binding. Weavers discovered anew that skeins of bound yarns fall in a different way than do ordinary skeins. Fiber is transformed by binding; it assumes a new range of characteristics. The stiffness of the bound areas alternating with the flexibility of the unbound areas makes the yarn move unexpectedly. The yarns themselves, just as they fall, create spatial volumes, often basket-like. Bound yarns were an obviously sculptural material.

36

Silk yarn tied with banana fiber in preparation for dyeing in the ikat process, Thailand. The many separate strands seem to create a single yarn bold in scale. Bound zones with their horizontal bindings interrupt the vertical movement of the multiple strands. The alternation of rigid and flexible areas forces the silk to fall into spatially open configurations, while the alternation of horizontal and vertical movements creates a visually active mass. (Collection of the Program in Visual Design, University of California, Berkeley.)

37

Woman's Festal Adornment, Afghanistan (detail). In movement the parallel yarns of plied wool bound with silk spring apart in a constantly changing definition of space.

38

Cameroon bag, raffia. The weaving of finely split raffia is outlined with plaiting and provided with a handle of many plied strands bound with raffia. The strands burst forth from the binding with great energy.

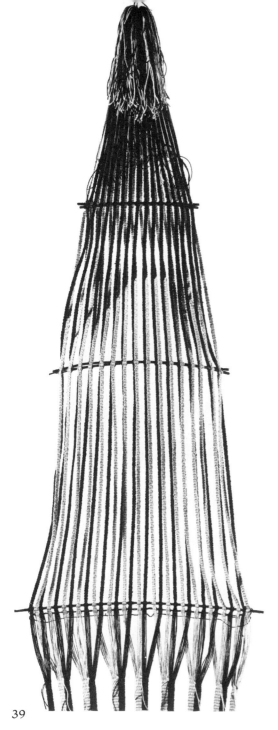

39

LENORE TAWNEY Wall Hanging of black
and natural linen, formerly in the collection of Dorothy Liebes. The yarns are
woven into strands of dark and light;
those on the lower surface change places
with those on the upper surface. The
effect is a movement backward and forward in space. The arrangement also
expresses the beauty of warps stretched
on a primitive loom—the shifting of
yarns forward and back as they cross
through the lease sticks. The woven
product seems to be at the same time
the loom.

The return to fiber in its raw state quite naturally
brought about investigation of weaving mechanisms
which seemed as down to earth as raw fiber and vegetable
dyes. The handweavers took a fresh look at their handlooms, which they recognized as machines similar to those
used in power production. Instead of conforming to the
loom any longer (Mary Atwater had admonished students
to work *with* the loom and to allow the loom to dictate), the
new weavers began to force the loom to serve new purposes. They improvised makeshift modifications to use the
standard loom in unorthodox ways. Sometimes they dispensed with the reed; other times they reduced the loom
to no more than a frame for stretching yarn. They turned
to primitive looms, frame looms, warp-weighted looms.
With simple looms the weavers experienced the satisfaction of being freed from a place and a piece of equipment.
The work could be done anywhere, under a tree or in front
of the television set. Weaving on these looms, with their
limitations and frustrations, was a sort of symbolic
gesture.

Often they rejected the loom entirely. They made their
work as clearly as possible a hand process. By turning
from the loom, fiberworkers were also turning from the
grid, the rectangular format often associated with the
static and decorative.

Freed from the loom, the individuals could think of
themselves as fiberworkers or fiber artists rather than as
handweavers. The loom could remain a useful mechanism
to be called upon as desired, but was no longer to be a
restrictive or determining force, conditioning all the
weaver's thoughts about fiber and its potentials. Today
many artists find that even the designation "fiberworker"
is a limitation to their expression. They are unwilling to be
bound to fiber. They are *artists*, free to explore in any
medium.

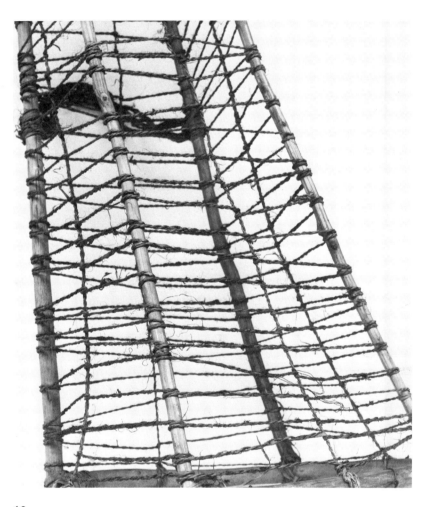

40

Mojave carrier, southern California. The rough cords move backward and forward between the sticks defining the volume of the crude basket. (Collection of Robert H. Lowie Museum of Anthropology, University of California, Berkeley.)

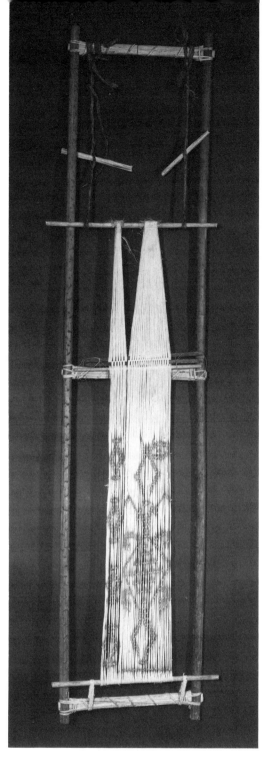

41

Loom, Borneo. The stretched warp has been patterned by ikat dyeing. The configuration of yarns is clearly recalled by Lenore Tawney's weaving. (Courtesy of the American Museum of Natural History.)

42

Pouch embroidered in silk and metal thread on canvas, French, fourteenth century. In their torn, worn, and frayed condition, textiles preserved from the past seem to declare their fibrous nature. In looking at ancient textiles, fiberworkers responded to this fibrous quality; they strived to achieve an assertion of fiber in their own work. (The Metropolitan Museum of Art, Gift of Mrs. Edward S. Harkness, 1927.)

Fiberworkers found structures appropriate to their materials and materials appropriate to their structures. A constant interaction resulted, quite unlike what happened with Contemporary handweavers whose structure was predetermined; for them material had to be adaptable to loom weaving for utilitarian textiles.

In another important way the new fiberworkers were unlike the Contemporary handweavers. The Contemporary weavers tended to see only their own work as they looked toward the future, whereas the new fiberworkers, through their explorations, became responsive to textiles of the past. They surrounded themselves with textiles which they loved and respected—the ancient handwork as well as the work still being produced in various parts of the world.

Weavers discovered that in any study of historical fragments of textiles, or even in looking at scraps from the recent past, what comes through is an awareness of the fibrousness. Frayed and faded, textiles declare their existence primarily as fiber.

Something else that became clear was the fact that in the long history of constructing with fiber, an immeasurable but certainly large percentage of the fiberwork was not primarily utilitarian, not protective clothing or shelter or workbaskets or whatever was regarded as useful fiberwork. Like clay and metal, fiber was a lively medium for art expression without qualifying conditions. In utilitarian objects left from the past, functionalism and expressiveness were often combined. Utilitarian objects were the vehicle for fiber expression; utility provided the occasion for—and stimulated—the expressive use of fiber. But when the utility was forgotten or ceased to operate, the art value remained, undeniable and compelling.

43

Mask, New Guinea Highlands. Basketry is
used to create lightweight but monumental shapes which are often daubed
with color and used as body adornments.
(Private collection.)

44, 45

Straw figure of the Virgin of Guadalupe, Mexico. Commonplace straw is worked into toys for children; it is also used to make religious figures for the home. The straw is twined and plaited in basic basketry techniques to become easily recognizable symbols. The straw has a remarkable glossiness which accentuates the various structures. Like silk yarn in satin weave and in embroidery, the straw is laid in parallel, unbroken lengths for maximum sheen.

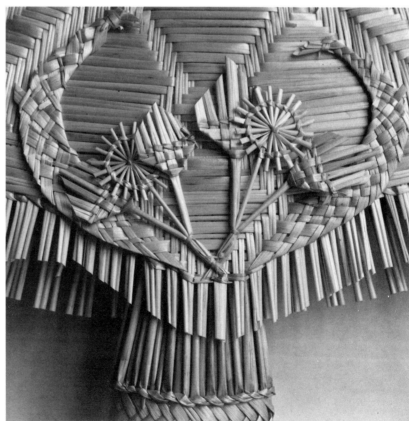

46

Facing Page:
WALTER NOTTINGHAM "Shrine." Manila and sisal rope, dyed jute, cotton, and linen are manipulated in the basketry techniques of coiling and twining to make a monumental shrine 8 feet high, 8 feet wide, and 2 feet deep.

47

TRUDE GUERMONPREZ "My Horizon."
The new fiberwork combines traditional
loom structures with hand manipulation
of yarns, and even extends to painting
the warps stretched on the loom, as a
vehicle for personal imagery. This wall
hanging is linen, wool and silk, dyed and
painted. (Syntex Corporation Collection.)

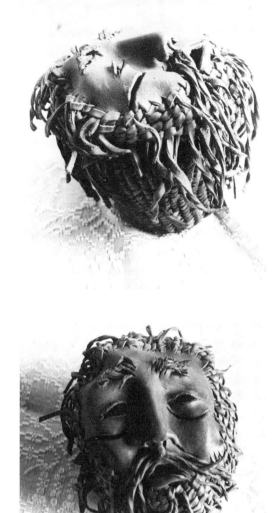

Handweavers realized that the essence of the machine textile product and the machine-like textile product is a repetition and a continuousness without beginning or ending. In their preoccupation with designing for the machine Contemporary weavers wove continuous lengths of machine-like fabrics—drapery, upholstery, suiting, casement cloth. They focused on the interior of a fabric to create all-over surfaces of color and texture.

In the new work beginning and endings were suddenly important. Units were unrepeated. Emphasis was on edges, bindings, knottings, and fringes. For a while handweaving was little more than a foundation to hold bindings, knottings, and fringes.

For guidance in solving problems of beginnings and endings handweavers turned to the work of nonindustrialized parts of the world, and to the fabrics of certain ancient cultures. The technical analyses of the cultural anthropologists became inspiration for new experiments with fiber.

48, 49

MARCIA FLOOR "Twined Masket." Leather is twined into a basket, topped with a leather mask slashed and raw, and encircled with a tangle of leather fringe.

50

Mescalero Apache basket with tin rattles, New Mexico. Just as woven textiles can be decorated with fringes, a basket can be elaborated with fringes, rattles, rag strips, etc., to sway when carried, and make the sounds of moving fiber, metal, glass, and shells to complement the sounds of the basket itself. (Collection of Robert H. Lowie Museum of Anthropology, University of California, Berkeley.)

Handweavers found that in many of the preindustrial societies nothing separated weaving from other textile techniques, even when one group of workers (for instance the men) did the weaving while another group (sometimes the women) did the knotting or embroidering. In their textiles a macramé fringe or other knotting terminated a woven length; or a row of twining functioned to space the warps for weaving; or embroidery stitches enhanced woven images. All the textile techniques were allowed to work together for an aesthetic purpose.

The Contemporary weaver's preoccupation with the power loom tended to separate the textile techniques and to foster a kind of specialization in thinking, a focus which encouraged the establishment and maintenance of boundaries. The new weaver, by studying a great number of ancient and preindustrial textiles, became aware of the bounty of techniques which did not involve the loom at all. Specialized and half-forgotten methods of constructing with fiber were suddenly intriguing.

51

Brown and white ikat rebozo, Ecuador. The shawl with its ikat cotton warp was woven on the loom and later the ends were knotted. Loom and nonloom techniques are matter-of-factly combined in a single piece. So marked is the contrast between the two areas—the woven and the knotted—it seems remarkable that the same warp yarns can create both. The diagonals of the knotting seem to flow from the strict horizontal-vertical of the woven section. (Courtesy of the American Museum of Natural History.)

52

Hat, Borneo. A basketry foundation is
overlaid with fiber strips appliquéd and
embroidered with cloth and metallic yarn.
Techniques and materials are freely
combined.

For a while fiberwork was without conditions, but soon new conditions appeared which recall what Dorothy Liebes said about weaving: handweaving is not an independent expression; it was *designed* to function in architectural settings.

New works in fiber began to be fabricated, just as paintings and sculptures were being fabricated, to enhance public buildings. Fiber artists worked with architects and decorators, agents and galleries, turning out monumental pieces to fit specific spots in public buildings. These fiber constructions were not designed to be machine produced or to fit the machine; rather they were to appear as one-of-a-kind hand products in relation to machine-culture environments.

To be in scale with such environments required a size out of easy range for an artist to produce alone. The size, the time, the expense, the technical involvements required a setting first. The work had to adapt to the conditions of the setting, since it was virtually inconceivable that a setting would be created for a work. Certainly a precedent existed in the European tapestries which are among the supreme expressions in fiber. Just as tapestries could not be produced except to order, or with a reasonable expectation of a sale, the new fiberworks in monumental scale could not be constructed without a commission.

With the new work, the fiber artist's role seemed to change. Large studios and assistants were required. Fiberworkers experienced a high sense of fulfillment working in architectural scale almost as a member of an architectural team. Liebes and the others had enjoyed the same satisfactions. Although the new fiber constructions were not functioning as casement cloths, upholsteries, and carpets, they were functioning to humanize and make livable vast and often cold and impersonal surfaces and volumes. Working in such scale imposed conditions upon fiberworkers, painters, and sculptors alike. Artists were willing to forego certain independence of expression accepting the conditions which allowed them to work large, to solve the sort of spatial problems which were so compelling at this time in the century.

53, 54, 55

SHEILA HICKS "Monde Mobile" (Labyrinth) (in process). Each warp and weft of white linen is a separate piece. The ends of each individual element are prominent features of the finished work. Construction of the noncontinuous elements is achieved without a loom. The short lengths are plaited as in mat-making and basketry. The ends of the elements are secured inconspicuously to preserve the direct statement of elements plaited. The result, a sort of fragment of woven structure seen under magnification, has a monumentality appropriate to large architectural volumes. Five panels interact together.

The new baskets which appeared concurrently with the new monumental works in fiber appear almost to be a reaction, so free are they of extrinsic considerations. The baskets are unattached, whole, self-sufficient. They retain direct relationship to individual persons, to the dimensions of the hand, to the size of the interior for living. Baskets are personal, intimate, approachable, able to be handled. They are in relation to a basketmaker, an observer, a user. These two expressions—the monumental fiberworks and the baskets—seem logical but antithetic outcomes of everything that happened in fiber.

When the new fiberworkers returned to raw fiber and to the exploration of constructions other than weaving—to experiment with fiber elements other than yarn, and to use nonloom techniques—they very quickly were working with basketry techniques. Sometimes they were using basketry techniques without making baskets, and sometimes they were making baskets without using basketry materials.

The Contemporary handweavers had been using some of the traditional hard fibers of basketry—bamboo, wooden dowels and slats, rattan—as rigid wefts in loom weavings for blinds and room dividers. Later weavers used these rigid wefts in wall hangings for their texture, size, and appealing contrast between the rigid and flexible.

Now with a freer, more experimental approach these hard fibers were manipulated off the loom. The resulting constructions were often basket-like if they were not actually baskets.

56

A bundle of raffia tightly bound at one end, with the fiber bursting forth energetically to form a great tassel.

58

Cordage in the studio of Barbara Shaw-croft. The heaped loops of glossy plied cord are spirited and rhythmic.

57

LILLIAN ELLIOTT Basket, blue raffia twined with multicolored yarns. The basket retains the beauty of the raffia bundle, enhanced by fine yarns which convert the bundle into a basket.

59

LILLIAN ELLIOTT Basket of paper twine with twined coconut fiber cord. The energetic paper twine, like a spring, is held with only occasional twining.

60

Hank of coconut fiber plied into cordage. Its dull dry surface seems to absorb light. The strands adhere together in a fibrous mass.

Many of the hard fibers of basketry resist being spun into continuous linear elements and they are insufficiently flexible to be knotted. So methods of construction were devised to allow the fibers to be joined in various degrees of compactness, and shaped. They are the basketry techniques—coiling, twining, plaiting, binding, etc.

61

Unfinished mat, Japan. Rags showing various indigo-printed patterns are twined along with rice straw which provides stiffness and also a contrast of fibers. (Collection of Robert H. Lowie Museum of Anthropology, University of California, Berkeley.)

62

NANCE O'BANION Rag basket (detail). Silk-screened cloth is torn into strips which cover stiff seagrass; the resulting elements are coiled with raffia as binder. Sometimes the rags hang free in series of fringes.

65

Inevitably, the thought and experimentation, the looking at textiles, and the making of textiles led to basketry. The new basketry did not evolve slowly and cautiously from the old. Certainly the old baskets were always there, remembered, exerting their influence. Even so, the new basketry was less of a development than it was a reinvention of baskets.

The new basketry tended to appear in parts of the world where basketmaking was no longer practiced and where no possibility existed of continuing a tradition or of learning the techniques in the old ways. The careful and precise instructions of the how-to-do-it books and the analyses of anthropologists were not the guides. The new basketmakers were unwilling to learn by making an identical copy of something from the past. Instead they were content to start with ordinary and familiar materials and manipulate them somehow into basket shapes. They took a simple technique such as twining or coiling and let something develop from the materials and technique.

63

Nineteenth-century embroidered basket, United States. It was fashionable to purchase baskets and decorate them with Berlin work in yarn. The basketry provided a canvas-like grid for working the patterns. (From *The Handcrafter*, January-February, 1930.)

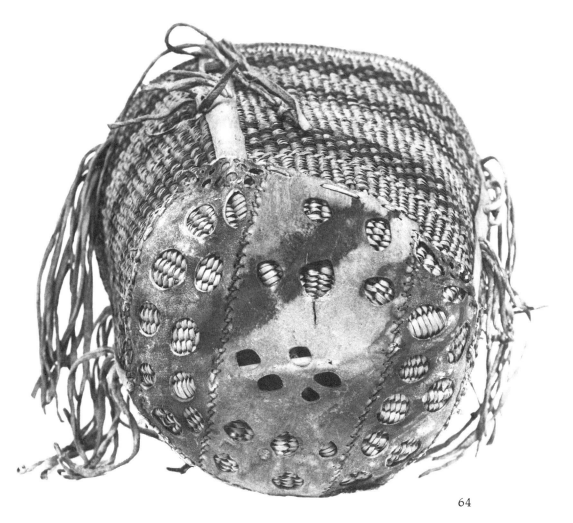

64

Twined basket, Mescalero Apache, New Mexico. Perforated leather is sewed to the basket's base. A leather fringe is attached. The effect is a combination of materials and a sense of layering—one thing seen through another. (Collection of Robert H. Lowie Museum of Anthropology, University of California, Berkeley.)

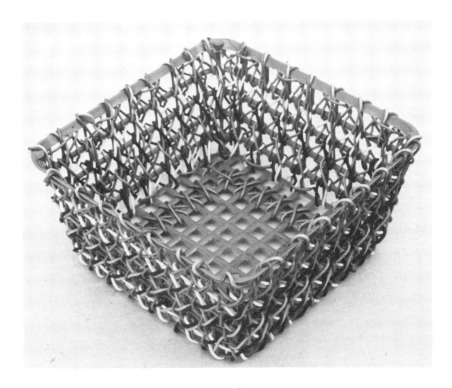

65

KATHERINE WESTPHAL Embroidered berry basket. The surface of a plastic berry basket is elaborated with colored telephone wire.

66

Riding cap, Nigeria. The exterior of the basketry is completely covered with leather, which is embellished with metal plates and leather fringe. (Collection of Robert H. Lowie Museum of Anthropology, University of California, Berkeley.)

67

Coiled storage basket from cave in Cuyama Mountains, California. A tear in the basketry was repaired with an insert and covered with pitch. Although the surprising combination of materials was utilitarian, it also functions aesthetically. (Collection of Robert H. Lowie Museum of Anthropology, University of California, Berkeley.)

68

MARCIA FLOOR "Sun in Leo, Moon in
Cancer." The basket is a mask, a head, a
presence. Twined and molded leather,
fur, and buttons are combined in a power-
ful emotional statement.

To many lovers of baskets the old ways were sufficient. Basketry did not need to change to be new and different. Change in basketry seemed to be shoving aside the old and discounting its values, just as industrial technology had shoved aside the hand processes in the other textile arts and transformed them. Change seemed inconsistent with the nature of basketry. Resistance to change and resistance to mechanization had seemed to be basketry's unique and commendable attributes.

Baskets which evolved out of weaving—or out of the various fiber activities which weaving stimulated—are different from other baskets. While basketry and weaving use the same constructional techniques, they use different materials—and materials have much to do with the appearance and nature of a structure. Rattan twined over rigid bamboo stakes is not at all like sisal cord twined over stakes of jute cord. When weavers began to manipulate the flexible and continuous yarns of weaving into basket shapes, what was most conspicuous was that the results lacked rigidity. Weavers tried everything to stiffen their baskets, which in many instances remained clothlike, malleable, subject to change. This softness became a conspicuous feature of much of the new basketry, imparting an irregular tipping, an uneasy balance, an uncertainty. Results seem to be hapless violations of the symmetrical and even of the functional. Not quite baskets and not quite bags, they defy clear classification and are therefore uncomfortable in a time preoccupied with classifications. While their softness makes them comfortably responsive to the touch, and allows them to accommodate to the weight and shape of things put into them, yet there is a sort of anxiety about them, a quality unknown in most commercial baskets. The same sort of anxiety is often evident in the new art fabrics which seem unresolved and uneasy, lacking any calm authority but instead imparting an undeniable sense of search and uncertainty.

69

Soft basket, Africa. Yarns of continuous
length replace the short traditional fibers
for both warp and weft. With such continuous elements a basket can be produced
more quickly for tourists.

70

Twined jar, Cuyama Mountains, California. The interior of the basket and the area surrounding the mouth are covered with pitch. Although the basket is rigid it appears soft and malleable and subject to change, like so much of the new basketry. This look in baskets was common in traditional work. (Collection of Robert H. Lowie Museum of Anthropology, University of California, Berkeley.)

71

JULIE ANDERSON Raffia basket with handle. The raffia is woven in strips of various widths sewed together into a basket. The handle and rim are stuffed, which increases the soft, bulky appearance.

72

72

JULIE ANDERSON Raffia basket. Woven
strips of raffia are interlaced and sewed
together into a soft, yielding basket.

73

INGER JENSEN Basket (detail). Bobbin-
lace techniques are used to construct this
basket. Elements are bound to stiffen
them.

The new basketmakers tend to use familiar, purchasable materials for their baskets, at the same time that they limit themselves to relatively few techniques. They use twine, yarn, raffia, rags, ribbon, tape, often with great ingenuity and invention. Techniques are mainly the simplest coiling, the simplest plaiting, and other simple yarn manipulations which are more often associated with soft textiles than with basketry: knotless netting, half-hitch knotting, continuous looping. Even weaving is used, with woven strips assembled into basket shapes.

74

Feathered hat, Tiahuanaco, Peru. The surface is imbricated with colorful feathers arranged in patterns solidly over the surface. (Courtesy of The Brooklyn Museum.)

75

Caps, Congo, Africa. Fiber is worked into a hard surface of nodules which are organized into swirling patterns. (Courtesy of the American Museum of Natural History.)

76

JOAN STERRENBURG "Wart Basket" (detail). Jute and linen yarns are knotted into a basket with an orderly arrangement of textural bumps which swirl around the basket in lively and playful fashion.

The new baskets differ from old baskets in their use of techniques and materials not formerly available. Textures and imagery are created with silk-screening and photographic processes. Plastic, television tape, etc., are used as structural materials. When formed into baskets these materials suggest that the artist looked at the modern world, perhaps as earlier people looked at surrounding vegetation, and matter-of-factly used what was available. To see movie film plaited into a basket which was traditionally made of palm strips encourages a new response to both the old and the new material. When the new basket-makers do use vegetal matter from surrounding nature they do not limit themselves to elements which have been proven useful in traditional baskets. They select materials for visual-emotional qualities quite unrelated to utility. They tend to avoid the hard fibers of bamboo and wood slats in favor of the softer, more flexible, materials.

77

MARTIÈ HOLMER Cloth basket. The basket is plaited from printed cotton cloth. The individual elements are carefully positioned to create patterns over the surface.

DOROTHY LIEBES Upholstery of plaited leather strips in green, brown, red, yellow, and orange. Liebes explored unconventional materials, and conventional materials in unexpected combinations, to satisfy utilitarian and decorative needs of the new interiors. (Collection of the Program in Visual Design, University of California, Berkeley.)

79

Bag, Eskimo. Translucent gut is pieced together; the seams and edges are embellished with wool stitching and feathers. (Collection of Department of Anthropology, University of California, Davis.)

80

MARY WINDER BAKER and NANCE
O'BANION Basket with gumballs. Polyethylene film and candy wrappers with
crimped edges provide translucent material for a playful basket.

81

NATASHA TORRES Plaited basket. The
traditional basket so often constructed
from ribbon-like strips of palm becomes
something new and provocative when
made from 8 mm. movie film. The white
film is leader.

82

MARY WINDER BAKER Plaited basket.
Plastic strips and metal foil create a glitter-
ing suspension of overlapping metallic
plates and translucent rectangles. The
plaiting and the spatial position of the
materials become equivocal.

83

Large storage basket of bamboo, Japan.
Strips of sturdy bamboo of various widths
interlace to create overlapping rectangular
shapes.

84

DEBRA RAPOPORT "Rainwear" (detail). Dyed paper tape is plaited and embellished with silk and metallic tassels.

85

Plaited basket (detail), Alaska. The traditional plaited ribbons of bark which are used in so much of the work of the Northwest Coast Indians are recalled in the plaited paper tape of Debra Rapoport's "Rainwear."

86

Shield, Tiahuanaco, Peru. A basketry
disk of split bamboo and cotton cord is
stretched with leather and painted. In its
present state the leather is perforated
irregularly, exposing the inner structure,
giving a sense of layering of materials
and patterns. (Courtesy of The Art In-
stitute of Chicago.)

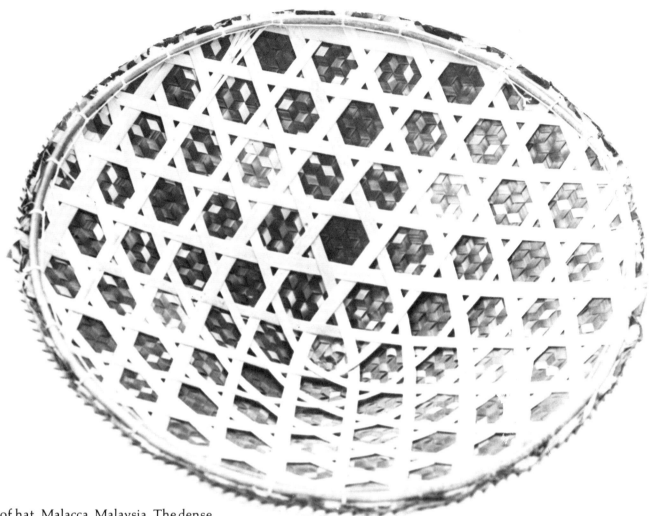

87

Inside of hat, Malacca, Malaysia. The dense exterior of colorful plaiting is supported by an open layer of bamboo strips. The effect is a layering of basketry, one structure partially concealing the other. The edge has a similar buildup of materials and techniques piled one upon the other. (Collection of Louise Barco Allrich.)

88

DEBRA RAPOPORT "Textured Layered Grid" (detail). Felted units are applied to wire mesh; mounds of jute fiber and yarns are applied horizontally, with sausage casings embellished with cloth and stitching undulating vertically over the mounds of fiber. A drawn grid on vinyl is applied to a wire mesh grid that also undulates as the top surface. The image of a grid is integrated with a structural grid as in Sue Venturino's plaited construction.

From the fiber upheaval of the fifties came a will to comprehend directly fiber expressions as a whole—except for those expressions which once had been done by hand but now were done by power machines.

The situation in basketry would seem not at all parallel since basketry was never mechanized. Yet the traditional basketmakers have possession of a vast area of basketmaking in the same way that power looms have possession of an immense part of weaving. The commercial basketmakers can not be competed with any more than can the power looms. The areas which remain for the handcraft basketmaker are not in the realm of the utilitarian but are exclusively in the realm of the nonutilitarian, the individual and artistically expressive.

At the same time that the new basketmaker eschews the making of baskets which are like the common run, he often avoids what seems machine-like—the meticulous modular repetitions which seem appropriate to a machine even though no machine is able to perform them and even though these are qualities most often admired in fine expressive baskets of the past.

The areas of weaving that were taken over by the power loom were those that seemed most "mechanical," most tedious in repetitiveness, and also most complex. The areas of basketry which are ignored by the new basketmakers are those that seem mechanical, tedious in their repetition, and technically intricate. The industrial revolution engendered attitudes toward work appropriate to the hand, and toward work that is worth spending time doing. Even though basketmaking was not mechanized, the new basketmaker is imbued with current attitudes toward mechanization which cause him to reject aspects of basketry which in many instances seem to be the very essence of the art.

Today boundless time is not usually squandered on constructing a single basket: results must come fast; an expenditure of time must show. The new basketmaker often calculates the value of an object in relation to the time spent making it—a consideration quite foreign to much traditional basketry. Just as baskets made for tourists by traditional basketmakers deviate from the ancient wares in their considerations of time and effort, so the new baskets show the same deviations but for somewhat different reasons. The making of tourist items is speeded up by using purchasable materials, often machine-made, ready dyed, in continuous elements. At times these materials are worked in traditional techniques, but at other times the techniques, like the materials, are modified for the sake of speed. The appearance of the old ware is merely recalled in the new product, often only faintly. The changed motivation of the basketmaker has led to changed materials and techniques. The results are often soft, casual appearing, sometimes incompetent. The tension created by the original materials is absent. Sometimes the result is a spontaneity and a pleasant sense of improvisation.

Although the new basketmaker is not motivated by the need for a fast result to survive, he is subject to the same pervasive influences. His need for a fast result is in the spirit of the time, in the vague pressures, the undefined values regarding time, repetitive processes, etc. The contemporary stresses are expressed in the new work— and consequently, this work often seems more akin to the deplored tourist items than to the quality baskets of the past.

The makers of the new baskets do not regard themselves as craftsmen or basketmakers in any traditional sense. Rather they are in most instances artists adept in various fiber skills who are finding in basketry one of the mediums for their expression.

Some workers in fiber create textile shapes which happen to resemble baskets; these creations are labeled "baskets."

Some workers set out to make baskets unencumbered by standard technical information. Their works, which are often intense and compelling, refuse to take the familiar basket shapes which spring so naturally from skill and traditional processes.

Some workers with sufficient skill to produce the conventional shapes are disgruntled when they see the conventional shapes evolving. This is not what they want to be doing. They arbitrarily disturb the order. They distort and violate the traditional.

Some workers proceed slowly and with deliberation, repeating old forms and techniques in untraditional materials. The effect is often as disturbing and arresting as are traditional fiber constructions when molded in plastic.

Some workers proceed with traditional materials in a kind of reverence, tuning in to the meditative aspects of the process, savoring the connections, resisting any innovation or strident effects, being motivated primarily by the doing, achieving a sort of anonymity in creating dateless, placeless artifacts. The working of fiber, the organizing of components, and the sensation of identity with tradition provide the satisfaction to the artist and to the observer.

Some workers feel that the essence of the new is in the total freedom from utilitarian considerations. Others believe that a basket is truly understood only through using it, and they therefore make only baskets which can be used.

One thing is certain: the new basketmakers are not attempting to revive traditional basketmaking, although they certainly are stimulating a new appreciation and awareness of the old. Nor are the new baskets made to replace those that are disappearing.

The new baskets are widening again a fiber field which became narrowed by pressures unrelated to the medium's expressive potentials. The sensuous qualities, the symbolic content, the references, the structural delights, the plastic nature of the medium are being rediscovered. Baskets are approached as abstract compositions of constructed volumes and planes, with attention given to implied spaces, all the relationships of open and closed, of penetrating forms, of inside and out. The new baskets suggest that structural problems are being solved for the first time, that materials are being used for the first time, that forms are evolving for the first time. The sensitive search is evident in the work.

PORTFOLIO OF THE NEW BASKETRY

89

JEORGIA ANDERSON Raffia basket, knotless netting.

90, 91

Facing page:
JULIE ANDERSON Raffia basket with handle.

STACY BAAR Basketry components,
twined seagrass.

93

JULIE ANDERSON Raffia basket.

94

STACY BAAR Twined construction
(detail). Jute.

95

MARY WINDER BAKER Plaited basket,
plastic.

96

CAROLINE VON KLEECK BEARD
Coiled basket of metallic gold thread.

97

LIA COOK Plaiting basket in her studio.

98

LIA COOK Plaited basket, cotton with photographic emulsion.

99

LILLIAN ELLIOTT Twined basket of
paper twine.

100

LILLIAN ELLIOTT Twined basket of
braided coconut fiber.

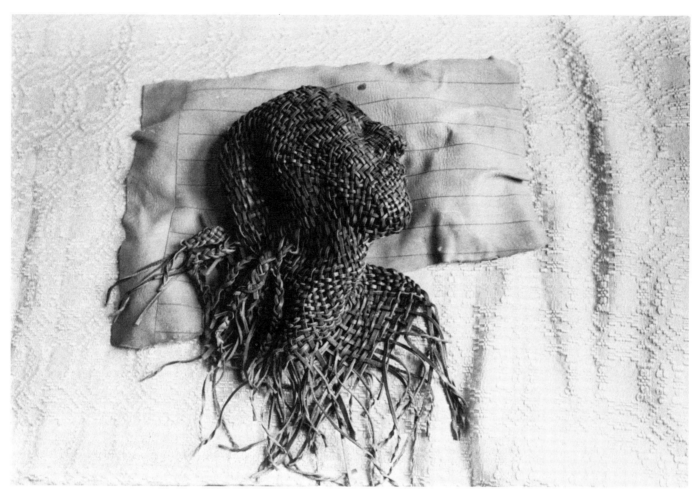

101

MARCIA FLOOR "Weaver Sleeper."
Plaited leather.

102

MARCIA FLOOR "Opening a Can of
Worms." Coiled and molded leather,
buttons, acrylic paint.

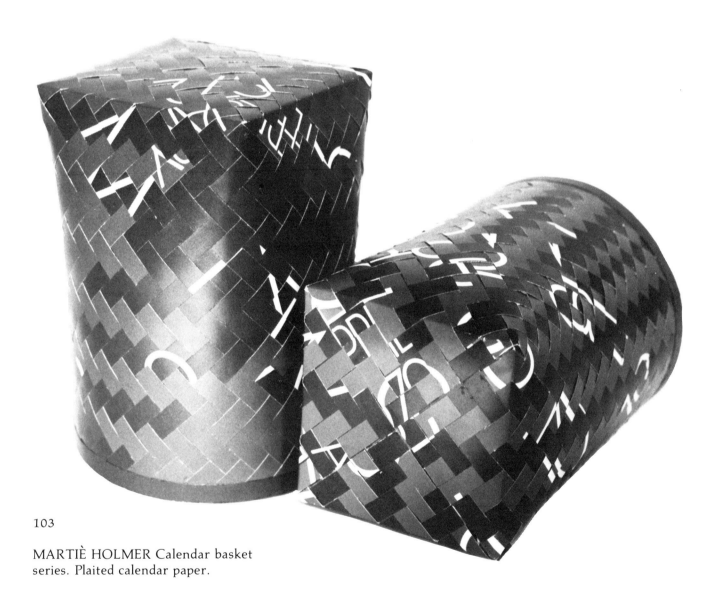

103

MARTIÈ HOLMER Calendar basket
series. Plaited calendar paper.

104

MARTIÈ HOLMER Covered basket,
plaited silk-screen print.

105

MARTIÈ HOLMER Cloth basket of
printed, folded, and plaited cotton cloth.

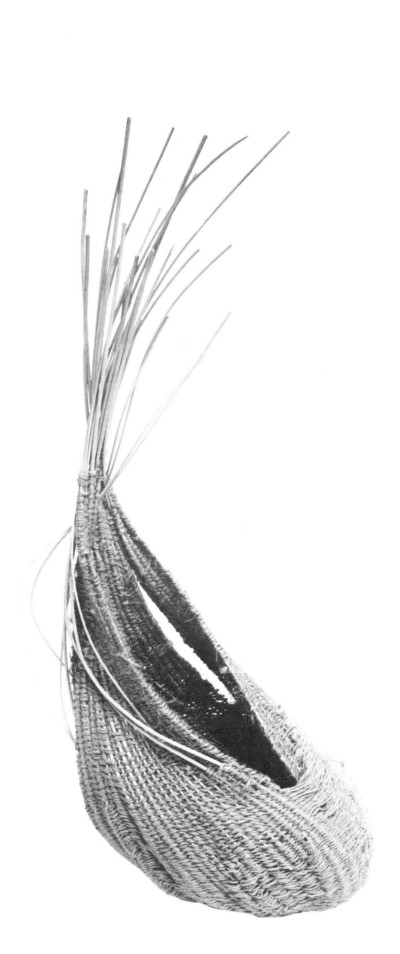

106

ROBERTA LOBBIN HOULLAHAN
Basket, hand-dyed sisal and bamboo.

107

ROBERTA LOBBIN HOULLAHAN
Basket, sisal, jute, and reed.

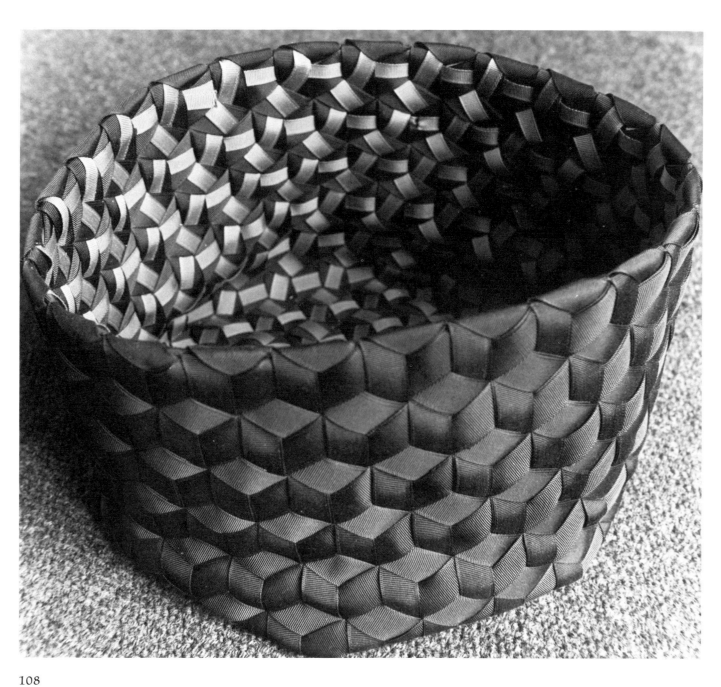

108

SUSAN JAMART Plaited basket, gros-
grain ribbon.

110

SUSAN JAMART Paper rush basket,
plaited.

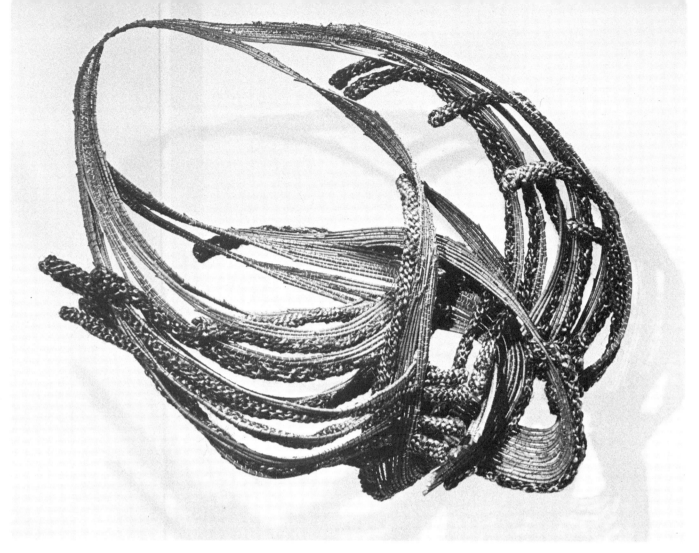

111

GYÖNGY LAKY "Mirror, Mirror." California sycamore twigs with telephone wire and plaited tubes of plastic and sisal tree rope. (Collection of Mrs. Dorothy S. Rudderman.)

112

GYÖNGY LAKY "Vernacular." The artist's assistant Laura Center is sitting inside. Handmade Guatemalan rope coiled with telephone wire.

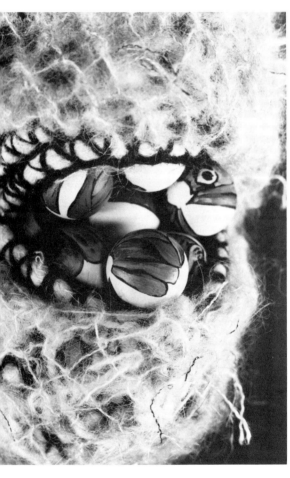

113, 114

LOIS LANCASTER Netted cocoon,
mohair. The interior is filled with painted
ping-pong balls which spill forth in
confusion.

115

AUGUSTA LUCAS Twined basket,
spun jute and jute roving over cotton
core.

116

AUGUSTA LUCAS Twined basket with
lid, unspun jute and jute roving.

105

Facing page:
CHERE MAH Plaited baskets of billboard
paper.

117

AUGUSTA LUCAS Twined basket, palm
stakes with New Zealand flax.

119, 120

NANCE O'BANION "Grass Basket." Silk-screened cotton, stuffed and coiled.

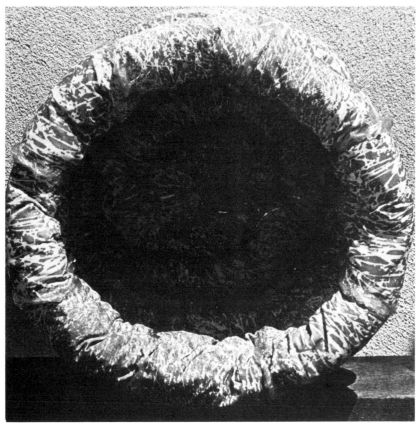

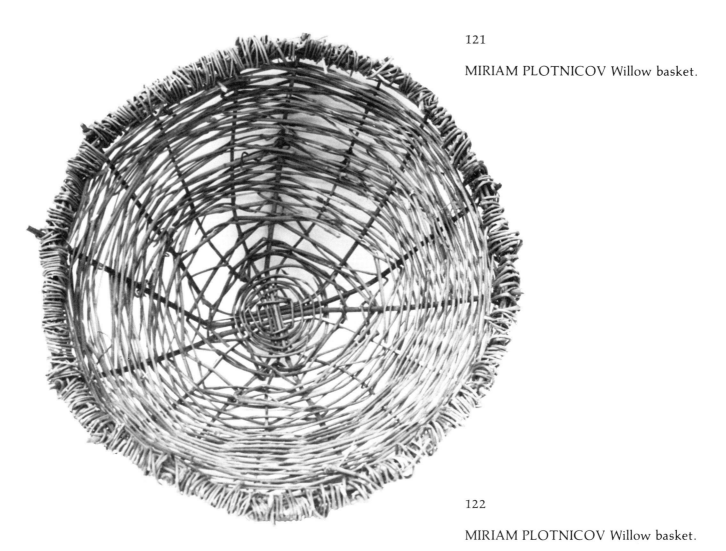

121

MIRIAM PLOTNICOV Willow basket.

122

MIRIAM PLOTNICOV Willow basket.

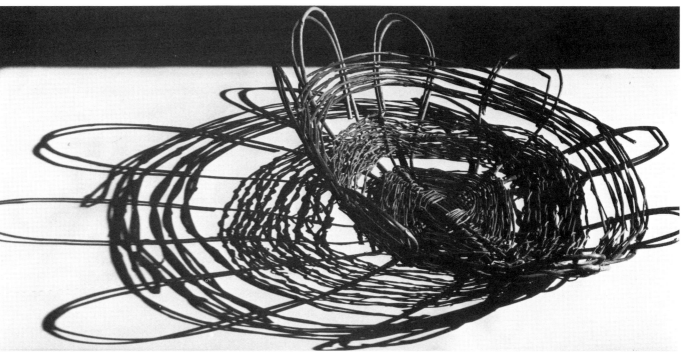

Facing page:
DEBRA RAPOPORT "Rainwear." Plaiting with dyed paper tape, cellophane, and ribbon tape.

123

ED ROSSBACH Bucket basket, coiled newspaper with polyethylene film.

125

ED ROSSBACH Twined basket,
newspaper.

126

ED ROSSBACH Netted bottles, cotton
and plastic.

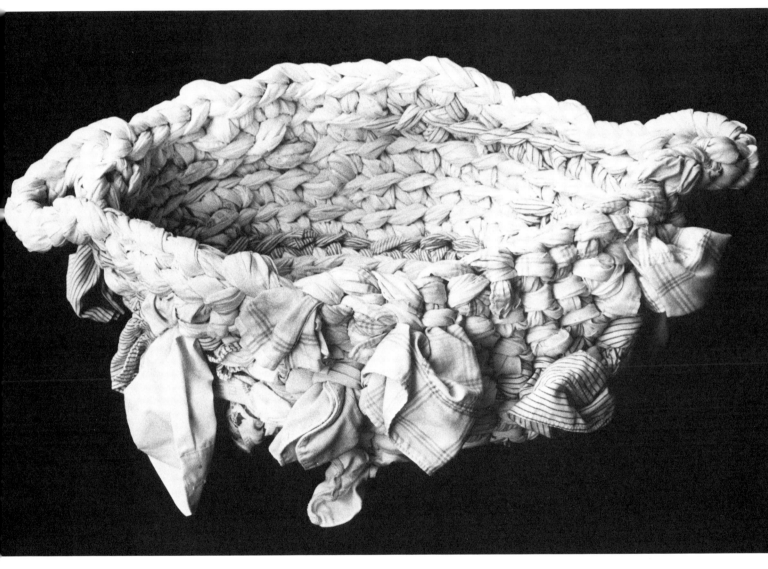

127

SUE VENTURINO "Laundry Basket."
Twined rags.

128

BARBARA SHAWCROFT Construction
in process, rope.

129

BARBARA SHAWCROFT Construction
in process, rope.

130

BUDD STALNAKER "Space Siphon,"
basket form, linen and polyethylene.
(Collection of R. Pfannebecker, Lancaster,
Pennsylvania.)

131

JOAN STERRENBURG "Wart Basket."
Knotted jute and linen.

CAROL SINTON Seaweed basket, netted.

133, 134

CAROL SINTON Seaweed basket, twined.

LUCY TRABER Twined basket, palm.

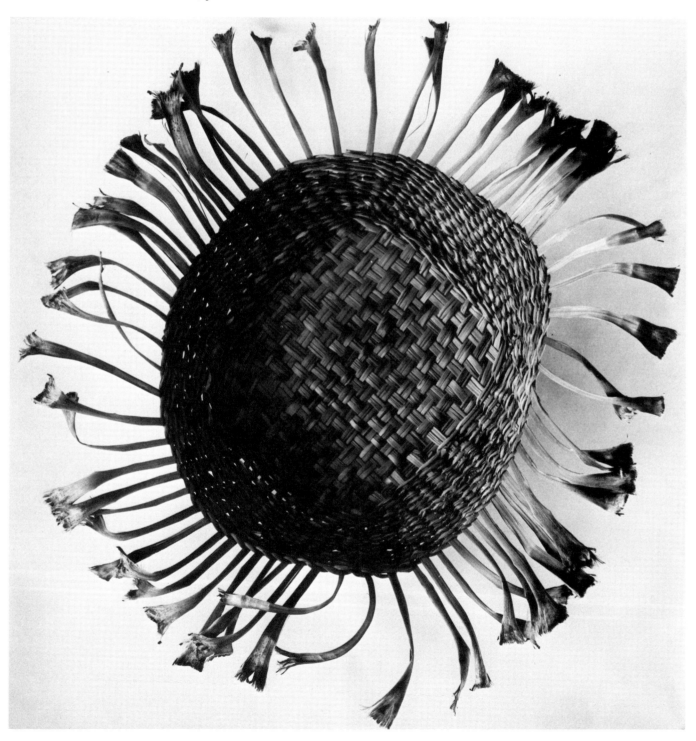

136

LUCY TRABER Seaweed basket, netted.

137

LUCY TRABER Seaweed basket with handle, twined.

138

GARY TRENTHAM "Swiss Linen Basket." Coiled, and fringed with knotted braids.

139

GARY TRENTHAM "Cotton Rope Basket." Coiled and knotted.

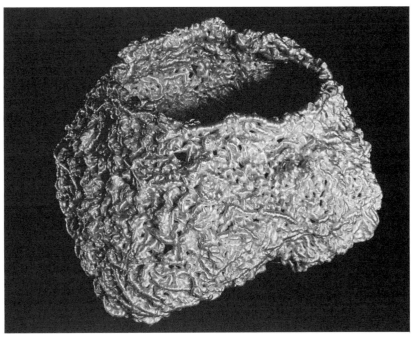

140

GARY TRENTHAM "Glad-Wrap Basket." Glad-Wrap material in random half-hitching.

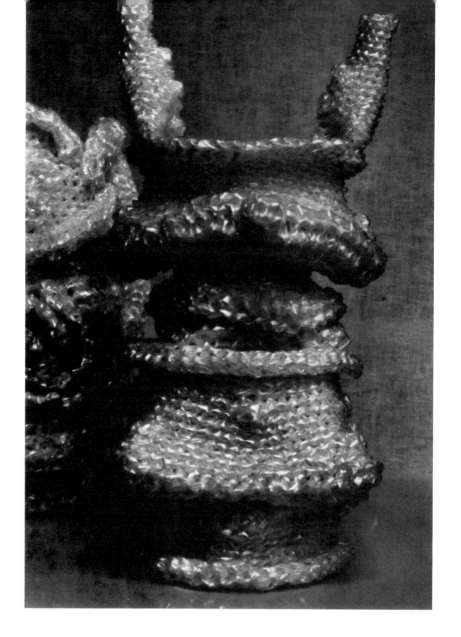

141

KATHERINE WESTPHAL Baskets, continuous looping of polyethylene tubing.

142

KATHERINE WESTPHAL Baskets, continuous looping of television tape, Mylar, and novelty rayon yarn.

143

KATHERINE WESTPHAL Baskets, continuous looping of television tape.

144

SUSAN WICK Knotted basket, plastic
tubing.

TEXT REFERENCES

Page 10   Irene Sargent, "Indian Basketry: Its Structure and Decoration," *The Craftsman*, Vol. VII, No. 3 (1904), p. 330.

Page 14   George S. Cole, *Cole's Encyclopedia of Dry Goods* (New York: Root Newspaper Assn., 1900), pp. 22–23.

Page 14   G. Glenn Lyman, "The Development of Basketry in the Public Schools," *The Philippine Craftsman*, Vol. V, No. 5 (Nov. 1916), p. 341 ff.

Page 15   Herbert D. Fisher, "Evolution of Industrial Supervision," *The Philippine Craftsman*, Vol. V, No. 1 (July 1916), pp. 85 ff.

Page 17   Sara Douglas Garbarini, *The Effect of Selected Technological Developments on the Structural Design of Machine Knitted Textiles*, unpublished MA thesis, University of California, Berkeley, 1969, p. 59, p. 73.

Page 19   "Revival of English Handicrafts: The Haslemere Industries," *The Craftsman*, Vol. I, No. 4 (Jan. 1902), p. 25.

Page 20   Peter Floud, "The Inconsistencies of William Morris," *The Listener*, October 14, 1954, p. 615.

Page 21   Mary M. Atwater, "A Primitive Weave," *The Weaver*, Vol. VI, No. 3 (July–Aug. 1941), p. 3.

Page 24   Navajo School of Indian Basketry, *Indian Basket Weaving* (New York: Dover Publications, Inc. 1971, republication of the work originally published by Whedon and Spreng Co., Los Angeles, in 1903), p. 8, p. 10.

Page 26   "Willow Baskets that Show the True Spirit of Handicraft," *The Craftsman*, Vol. XVIII, No. 2 (May 1910), p. 264.

Page 26   Irene Sargent, "Indian Basketry: Its Structure and Decoration," *The Craftsman*, Vol. VII, No. 3 (December 1904), p. 321.

Page 28   Anni Albers, "Handweaving Today," *The Weaver*, Vol. VI, No. 1 (Jan-Feb. 1941), p. 3.

Page 29   William Morris, *The Collected Works of William Morris*, Vol. XXII, "Some Hints on Pattern Designing," 1881 (New York: Longmans, Green & Co., 1910–1915), p. 182.

Page 32   Bernard Chaet, *Artists at Work* (Cambridge, Mass.: Webb Books, Inc., 1960), p. 65

Page 38   Anni Albers, "Work with Materials," Black Mountain College Bulletin 5.

Page 50   Mary M. Atwater, "It's Pretty—but is it Art?" *The Weaver*, Vol. VI, No. 3 (July-Aug. 1941), p. 14.

Page 60   Dorothy Wright Liebes, "Modern Textiles," *Decorative Arts*, Official Catalog, Dept. of Fine Arts, Division of Decorative Arts, Golden Gate International Exposition, San Francisco, 1939 (San Francisco: H. S. Crocker Co., Inc., Schwabacher-Frey Co., 1939).

BIBLIOGRAPHY

Anni Albers, *On Designing* (Middletown, Conn.: Wesleyan University Press, 1971).

———, *On Weaving* (Middletown, Conn.: Wesleyan University Press, 1974).

Arts and Crafts Movement in America 1876–1916, edited by Robert Judson Clark (Princeton, New Jersey: Princeton University Press, 1972).

Mary Meigs Atwater, *The Shuttle-craft Book of American Hand-Weaving* (New York: The Macmillan Co., 1928).

Bauhaus (1919–) 1928, edited by Herbert Bayer, Walter Gropius (and) Ise Gropius (New York: Museum of Modern Art, 1938).

Ella Shannon Bowles, *Homespun Handicrafts* (Philadelphia: J. B. Lippincott Company, 1931).

Denis Diderot, *Planches pour l'Encyclopédie, ou pour le Dictionnaire raisonné des sciences, des arts et des métiers* (1765–76).

Allen H. Easton, *Handicrafts of the Southern Highlands* (New York: Dover Publications, Inc., 1973).

Fifty Years Bauhaus, Catalog of German Exhibition sponsored by the Federal Republic of Germany (Pasadena, Cal.: Pasadena Art Museum, 1970).

Charles Coulston Gillispie, *A Diderot Pictorial Encyclopedia of Trades and Industry* (New York, 1959).

Edgar Kaufmann, Jr., *What is Modern Design?* (New York: The Museum of Modern Art, 1950).

William Morris, *Hopes and Fears for Art* (New York: Longmans, Green, 1908).

Gilliam Naylor, *The Arts and Crafts Movement* (Cambridge, Mass.: The MIT Press, 1971).

Herbert Read, *Art and Industry* (New York: Harcourt, Brace and Company, 1938).

Walter Scheidig, *Crafts of the Weimar Bauhaus* (New York: Reinhold Publ. Corp., 1967).

INDEX

Boldface numbers refer to illustrations.